BATTERED
INTO
SUBMISSION

THE TRAGEDY
OF WIFE ABUSE
IN THE
CHRISTIAN
HOME

James Alsdurf
& Phyllis Alsdurf

INTERVARSITY PRESS
DOWNERS GROVE, ILLINOIS 60515

InterVarsity Press is the book-publishing division of InterVarsity Christian Fellowship, a student movement active on campus at hundreds of universities, colleges and schools of nursing. For information about local and regional activities, write Public Relations Dept., InterVarsity Christian Fellowship, 6400 Schroeder Rd., P.O. Box 7895, Madison, WI 53707-7895.

All Scripture quotations, unless otherwise indicated, are from the Holy Bible, New International Version. Copyright © 1973, 1978, International Bible Society. Used by permission of Zondervan Bible Publishers.

Cover illustration: Roberta Polfus

ISBN 0-8308-1263-6
Printed in the United States of America

Library of Congress Cataloging-in-Publication Data

Alsdurf, James, 1951-
  Battered into submission.

  Bibliography: p.
  1. Wife abuse—Religious aspects—Christianity.
2. Wife abuse—United States.   3. Women, Christian—
United States—Abuse of.   4. Church work with abused women—United States.   I. Alsdurf,
Phyllis, 1950-
II. Title.
HV6626.A48   1989   362.82'92575'0973   89-15347
ISBN 0-8308-1263-6

---

17   16   15   14   13   12   11   10   9   8   7   6   5   4   3
99   98   97   96   95   94   93

for Lucy

Acknowledgments

Writing this book has been an arduous task that has spanned eight years. Our primary debt, of course, is to the many women and several men who have shared with us their stories that had been laid to rest, recounting painful memories in the hope that others might be helped. Many have encouraged us along the way, including Rob and Anne Johnston, who first challenged us to investigate this matter; Ginny Booth and the staff of *Family Life Today* magazine, who were extremely helpful in the data-gathering phase; and Newton Maloney and Jim's dissertation committee at Fuller Seminary's School of Psychology, who gave helpful direction for the initial research.

Margo Goldsmith provided special support at a point when we were ready to abandon the project. Connie Doran shared openly from the insights she had gleaned from her work with battered women. Betty Evans-Wells was instrumental in connecting us with a number of women whose stories needed to be heard. John Wilson, Margaret Koch and Mary Byers critically read various drafts of the manuscript and helped us think through the issues.

The teaching and spiritual insight of our pastors, Jack Hayford, Don Pickerell and William Lane, helped us formulate an understanding of the problem of evil as it relates to wife abuse. Catherine Kroeger, Alvera and Berkeley Mickelsen, and many faithful friends in Christians for Biblical Equality have encouraged us in this difficult work and demonstrated a commitment to seeing women and men set free. Throughout the process we have been faithfully undergirded by the prayers of many, among them those of Linda Brooks and Frank and Lorraine Alsdurf.

Finally, our children—Hannah, Benjamin and Lydia—have grown up eagerly waiting "until the book is done." They have shared in the struggle and the sense of purpose it has provided for our family.

Introduction:
Trouble in
Paradise

Eight years ago we were not aware that wife abuse even occurred in Christian homes. Then in 1981 we were brought face-to-face with the matter. As editor of *Family Life Today* magazine, Phyllis prepared an article on wife abuse in Christian homes. As she talked with several women who found the courage to tell their stories, she was stunned by the extent of the problem. Wives told of being struck in the face, kicked, bruised, dragged across the floor by their hair, and even bitten. And by whom? Ordained ministers, Christian businessmen, some well-known evangelical leaders—all men who lived a lie and perpetrated abuse that was an abomination to God.

After learning of one woman's story, *Family Life Today* published a special section of articles on wife abuse, inviting Christian women who were victims to respond. Over sixty women did so, many of them vividly detailing their pain-filled marriages. And the letters that came from those battered women—*Christian* women—convinced us that wife abuse was indeed a problem in Christian homes.

Today, wife abuse has come to the forefront of society's concerns. Numerous books and services address the subject, many aimed at Christians. Yet we have an abiding concern, influenced by the persisting stories we still hear: though some externals have changed, the attitudes remain the same. People have learned what to say, but their actions do not match their words.

We are convinced that God called us to be advocates for battered Christian women, a group that has been a powerless minority. But confronting the principalities of darkness which foster this insidious violence has meant experiencing spiritual warfare as never before. We have often been tempted to abandon this task; then another battered woman would come into our lives. So we continue our investigation into the issue with these words as our theme: "For the vision is yet for the appointed time; it hastens toward the goal, and it will not fail. Though it tarries, wait for it; for it will certainly come, it will not delay. Behold, as for the proud one, his soul is not right within him; but the righteous will live by his faith" (Hab 2:3-4 NASB).

As we have worked in this area we have felt outrage that violence of this sort occurs as frequently as it does in Christian homes and that it so often goes unchallenged by the church. In fact, the church has at times contributed to the mistreatment of women through complacency, insensitivity and its imbalanced teachings on male-female roles.

Whatever form brutality takes, the fact that it exists unchecked in Christian homes is a deep affront to our faith. To consider the problem of wife abuse in Christian homes—beyond the serious theological and psychological issues—we must consider the church's fundamental attitude toward and treatment of women.

Our aim in writing this book has been to listen not only to abused women, but also to those in positions of church leadership. We want to consider some of the theological and psychological concerns at stake. We hope that by looking broadly at the problem of wife abuse and examining its impact on the whole Christian community, practical ideas for intervention and ministry will come to light.

Wife abuse is a problem we dare not ignore. We must learn how and why wife abuse occurs in Christian homes, and we must grasp what it is telling us about our view of marriage and male-female relationships. For there is trouble in paradise.

How long, O LORD, must I call for help, but you do not listen? Or cry out to you, "Violence!" but you do not save? Why do you make me look at injustice? Why do you tolerate wrong? Destruction and violence are before me; there is strife, and conflict abounds.

Habakkuk 1:2-3

1
A
Nightmare
in the
Christian Home

escribed as a "saintly character," she was thirty-one years old,
a devoutly Christian woman and the mother of five children.
But this Baptist pastor's wife said she just "couldn't take it
anymore." So she shot and killed her husband of fourteen years,
the man she said had repeatedly abused and threatened to kill
her and their children.

In a landmark Minnesota decision in March of 1984, Lucille Tisland
was acquitted of the murder. Said one juror after the trial: "It was
probably the hardest thing I ever had to do—not making the decision
but hearing the heartbreaking testimony."[1]

Robert Tisland, described as a mesmerizing, pulpit-pounding
preacher, schooled his wife and children in unwavering subjection to

his tyrannical demands. The children were beaten with regularity because, Lucy said, "he expected perfection from all of us." Even included in those beatings was twenty-five-pound, seven-year-old Mark, left blind, deaf and brain-damaged from a stroke. Dying of encephalitis, the child held a special place in Lucy's heart. Managing his fourteen-hour-a-day schedule was solely up to her.

On May 4, 1983, Mark died and Robert was relieved. Mark was an "imperfect child," he reasoned, and Lucy had been responsible for his illness because of some sin she had committed. So, when she went into the bedroom to cry over the loss, he beat her and then again on the way home from the funeral.

"I was afraid," Lucy acknowledged. "If he had told me to jump off a bridge, I would have done it. One of his sayings was, 'It's not yours to question why. It's yours to do or die.' I was always taught that divorce was wrong—once married, always married."

In fourteen years of marriage, Lucy was pregnant nine times and the family moved nineteen times. "He didn't consult anyone," she recalled without emotion. "He was my husband, and I knew I was supposed to follow his decisions. You get married and the Bible says you are to obey your husband. Right from the start he was the boss."

Lucy had two books as her guide—*Woman the Completer* by Jack Hyles and *Me, Obey Him?* by Elizabeth Rice Handford—books she had read three or four times. "They outline the role of the woman and give the man rulership," she said. "I've lived that passage from Ephesians— 'Wives, be subject to your husbands as unto the Lord.' That was his main verse."

And her role was abundantly clear. "Women could stay home and have kids. We were supposed to be there to meet our husbands' needs. That meant obeying my husband and that his decisions were final. I believed that. To not believe that was to be disobedient to God and to my husband."

The beatings, which began ten months after their marriage and during her first pregnancy, were always in response to Lucy's lack of submissiveness, Robert told her. Despite the violence he bragged that there were no problems in their marriage. After all, his wife did all the cleaning and baking, polished his shoes, hung up his clothes and served him his food, which he was free to dump on the floor if it in any way displeased him. She never left the house without checking with him, didn't drive without his permission and had only ten to twenty-five cents in her possession for a phone call. Lucy never wore slacks or make-up, except when he permitted it in order to cover a bruise. And although he was her husband, Robert was referred to by Lucy as "Pastor" or "Sir."

But one day Robert Tisland came home at an emotional breaking point from the Christian school he directed. His questionable relationship with a fourteen-year-old girl had been found out. The week had been a "nightmare of beatings" for the family; he had already beaten Lucy three times that day.

Robert said that after napping he intended to kill Lucy. She knew he meant it. He always followed through on his threats, she claimed, and frequently took naps before beating her. "He was carrying on like a crazy person," Lucy said during the trial. "His eyes were wild. I had never seen him look like that. I had never seen anyone look like that. He said that he was at the breaking point, that I would not see another morning and that he was going to kill me."

As Robert slept, Lucy slipped out the loaded .22 he always kept under his pillow. "He opened his eyes and acted like he was going to sit up. . . . I sat up and I shot him." Then she took the boys to a friend's house, returned home and called the sheriff.

Why did Lucy and the boys keep the horror of their family life a secret for so many years? Because they feared and loved Robert Tisland, they said. And, as Lucy testified, "I was scared of leaving because he had threatened that if I ever left he would come and find me and the boys, and all that would be left would be pieces."

Committed Christians, Traditional Values

Wife abuse. The Christian home. Two terms that should be mutually exclusive. Tragically, however, they are not. While the Tisland case is extreme, it is not isolated. In the past eight years we have met and talked with many "Lucys," women whose situations have been less well publicized, generally less severe, but no less heart-rending. For a regrettable number, emotional instability and spiritual confusion remain long after the physical bruises have faded. A Minnesota woman, divorced for eight years after a twenty-year abusive marriage, noted, "Even after all these years I still suffer from the mental abuse. He kept telling me I was dumb all the time and I believed it. Even now I feel like I can't make it."

Wives are not the only ones wronged. They are the mothers of children who are often petrified of their fathers and who may have been sexually molested and physically abused. Some are boys, "spitting images" of their fathers, already manifesting his ways of dealing with anger and relating to women by beating up their girlfriends—or their mothers. And there are the girls, programmed at an early age to believe that men have the right to demean and victimize women.

Wife abuse doesn't occur just in families in which husbands are unsaved or alcoholics, where mothers work outside the home or couples are only nominally Christian. Many of the abused women with whom we talked are married to church leaders, deacons or pastors. They all consider themselves to be committed Christians and for the most part would uphold traditional family values. Few would label themselves feminists, and almost without exception they have worked hard at being submissive to their husbands.

The majority of women in our sample were in their first marriage, had children, received some college education (almost fifty per cent had graduated), held a part-time job and were in good physical health. The families in which they grew up could best be described as average American families: "very religious," stable (only about ten per cent had parents who were divorced or separated), relatively violence-free and middle-class.

What, in these Christian homes, was conducive to abuse? The findings of researchers Christy Telch and Carol Linquist give an important clue. They determined that violent couples "have more stereotyped sex-role attitudes and more traditional views of marriage."[2] When a very legalistic, highly traditional world view is adopted by men who have "exaggerated needs for dominance vis-à-vis their wives, poor verbal skills to enable them to establish such dominance, poor access to their emotions, exaggerated anxiety about relationship issues" and difficulty with intimacy, such factors can provide fertile ground for the emergence of violent behavior.[3]

The distribution of power can be badly skewed in the Christian home. Fortified by preaching that accepts all sorts of cultural assumptions about what "headship" means, abusers often use Scripture as ammunition for their misuse of power. One battered wife noted, "While the hierarchy of marriage can produce profound humility in some men, in others it can be fuel to flames of dominance and even violence. Wives of such men, obedient to their misconception of submission, often reinforce their husbands' violent or antisocial behavior."

That same woman describes her marital situation and the church's failure to confront her husband's sin:

After marriage my husband treated me as a nonperson with no value other than through him. He cited Scripture passages in support of his treatment of me. Any time I objected to his behavior or to his decisions, he told me that I was to submit to him just as totally as if he were Jesus Christ. He firmly believed that if I were obedient and submissive, God himself would take care of me. Therefore he was free to behave as irresponsibly as he liked without fear of hurting me or our child. He felt God wouldn't allow us to be hurt unless it was God's will.

My husband took no responsibility for his actions at all. I spent many agonizing hours in prayer and fasting, seeking to drive out every vestige of sin from my life. I believed that when I finally learned what God was trying to teach me, my husband would respond with love. But the more I submitted to him, the more arrogantly he displayed his flagrant abusive behavior. I sought counsel from pastors and friends. Many didn't believe me. It's not hard to understand why. How could such an upstanding member of the church and community be capable of such a miscarriage of God's justice?

I despised his attendance and eager participation at church because it underlined the contrast to his behavior at home. Those who did believe me offered no solace; only sympathy and empty platitudes. They affirmed my submissive reaction to my husband's abusive tyranny. No one at any time went to talk to my husband about his behavior in loving correction. I was always left empty-handed to return to my personal hell.

In those circles where wives are taught to submit blindly to their husbands' every word and deed, where divorce is preached against without consideration of the circumstances involved, and where dominance by the husband is seen as his "divine right" and responsibility, the sin of wife abuse can exist unchecked. In fact, such teachings provide a good covering for abuse under the guise of bringing one's wife "into subjection." Thus the batterer does not consider his actions abusive; he is simply fulfilling his God-given responsibilities.

Recognizing Abuse as Sin

A first and difficult step in working with abusers is getting them to acknowledge that what they have done is wrong. In a Christian setting that problem is compounded by church leaders who are afraid to confront the perpetrator with his sin.

Take, for example, the situation of Ann and Scott. At forty-five years of age, Ann is an attractive, athletic woman. Vivacious and outgoing, she is someone who has committed half of her life to a youth ministry and as many years to trying to "fix" her marriage. Scott is articulate and bright, leadership material. Fittingly, he has been involved in Christian ministry for years. And he is abusive.

The physical abuse started on their honeymoon; the verbal abuse was unceasing. "I never lived up to his standards," said Ann. "In his eyes I wasn't a good cook or housekeeper or lover. And as our children became old enough to express opinions it became more evident that I also was a crummy mother."

In their conservative Christian world, "divorce or separation is not a consideration," Ann said. "Besides, divorce admits failure, and I was really optimistic that things would get better if I worked harder, tried to please Scott more, to do and be what he wanted." Only when the abuse was directed toward her children did Ann take action.

There were the violent outbursts, way out of proportion to any wrong done, and constant verbal abuse. And then there were Scott's disturbing obsessions. His nightly routine with the children, for instance, was "humiliating and violent" and continued on into the junior-high years. He scrubbed the children's faces until the girls cried and then flossed their teeth until their gums bled. Everyone walked on eggshells at home, disappearing into their rooms when Scott came home.

"I never dared admit the abuse because once I pulled my head out of the sand and admitted it, I knew I'd have to do something about it," said Ann. Then her thirteen-year-old confronted her. "Every day Dad treats you like s--- and you let him," she said. Ann was shocked. "I had never heard her say that word. Then I felt embarrassed, humiliated. My kids had seen the abuse and called it before I did."

One Mother's Day the situation came to a head. "Sundays were always the worst day of the week," Ann noted. "But this Sunday was worse than usual." Scott ritualistically lined the children up and, for an hour, recited Ann's failings. "The kids were terrorized," Ann recalled. "They were crying as he talked. I was pacing in the next room, talking to the Lord. Scott had forbidden me to come in. We were in fear of our lives, and we absolutely felt that he could kill us. He told me he hated me."

Then Scott started in on the children, calling the oldest girl a slob. When he hit her across the face, something in Ann snapped. "That was it. I couldn't stop. I was fearless. I chased him around the house. Just let him try to hit me. I would have killed him." That afternoon she and the children left.

Later, she tried to work at reconciliation with Scott, but "he never apologized, *never,* not once in twenty-three years. I knew it was hopeless when he told me, 'What you don't understand is that not everybody thinks it's bad.' I said the only ones who don't think abuse is bad are those doing the abusing."

Ann still struggles with the fact of divorce. "In my heart I know I did the right thing. But part of me thinks maybe I should have stayed separated forever."

And when she tried, through one of the church elders, to contact her pastor for help, Ann was totally discounted. "The pastor called in his secretary and dictated a letter to Scott saying he and the elders would meet with him. Scott ignored it, and I was never called or contacted. I was a nonperson, a woman."

Ann's experiences point to an all-too-common struggle for women whose abusive husbands have been given tacit permission by the church to continue their abuse. When this happens, the wives are ignored, left to suffer in silence.

The Response of Clergy

A 1979 survey of eighty-one abused women by Cheryl Ellsworth and Irene Wagner found that eighteen per cent sought help from clergy, but only half of those were satisfied with the response they received.[4] Victims' attempts to enlist counsel from pastors have resulted in feelings of guilt, condemnation or responsibility for the conflict.[5]

In *The Family Secret*, sociologists William Stacey and Anson Shupe report on their two-year study of wife abuse. With regard to the role of the clergy in wife abuse cases, they note:

> The sad fact is that ministers and priests are currently much better at marrying men and women than they are at dealing with spouse abuse. We have yet to talk to a woman who felt she received much aid from a clergyman. A number of women were quite bitter about their futile attempts to get clergy to help.[6]

Why is this so? Because, Stacey and Shupe contend,

> the clergy have traditionally had powerful reasons to minimize family violence as a problem in their congregations. The family is, after all, the bedrock underlying most churches. . . . To confront violence in an otherwise respectable family reflects poorly on the mission and ideals of a church. It also reflects indirectly on the effectiveness of the minister as the shepherd of his flock.[7]

These researchers also found that the response of clergy varied depending on the denomination or church.

> Women in Roman Catholic, Greek Orthodox, and conservative Protestant churches (such as the Church of Christ, the Southern Baptist Church, and various fundamentalist denominations) are most likely to find their priests or ministers of little help. The kinds of family conflict that might lead to divorce or separation threaten these groups. Their clergy are likely to recall the admonitions of Saint Paul on controlling women and use them to justify telling the woman she must stay in the abusive home. Here women will probably be counseled by a minister to "try to be a better wife" or to "be more considerate of him" and "obey him." Leaving the abusive marriage, or divorcing him, will be branded desertion or a sin, shifting the blame to her. In short, if she is a churchgoing battered woman her chances of getting meaningful ministerial help are better in churches of a more moderate-to-liberal persuasion such as

Methodist, Presbyterian, Episcopalian, or Unitarian.[8]

A few of the women with whom we've talked praised their churches and pastors for their efforts at intervention. Said a woman from the East Coast, "One of the reasons that mine is a 'success' story—my husband and I are back together after a three-month separation—is because my church did take action. It forced my husband to make choices and he sought counsel himself."

Another woman found that pastoral counsel varied greatly in the two churches she attended. "The first pastor I talked to focused on keeping the family together. The others had a more realistic and (now I believe) spiritual approach. They advised separation for as long as it takes to make a wise decision and to see if my husband is truly willing to change. . . . The pastors were committed to finding me a place to stay. . . . They have also loved and cared for my husband. One pastor has confronted him in love and has been involved in helping him change."

Unfortunately, most of the pastors who counseled the women we've interviewed viewed the problem primarily in spiritual terms, simplifying the psychological, familial and social complexities involved. Women report being advised to consider the abuse "an opportunity to suffer for Jesus' sake."

"The pastor put the guilt on my shoulders," a Florida woman told us. "He blamed me for not submitting to my husband and said that my husband would change because he had asked for forgiveness. But after counseling I realized he would never change; he was more abusive than ever. In a sense the pastor was on my husband's side. I was showing little faith, he said. This minister even knew that my husband was making sexual advances to my daughter."

A woman who rates the abuse she has experienced in her ten years of marriage as severe ("I thought I'd die"), wrote that a Christian counselor she saw said, " 'You have to forgive totally and commit yourself 100 per cent'—which I can't—'before God can work on your husband.'. . . He very strongly emphasized that I am to obey my husband despite the violence because I'm really obeying God when I do this, and I need to die to self and see Christ as my all."

Many of the women perceived their pastors as naive or fearful of getting involved in abuse cases, particularly with husbands who hold positions of power within the church. A woman, first abused on her honeymoon, claims she is beaten "continuously, every day lately," by her husband of twenty-five years. While her pastor and the church board did confront her deacon husband, the main focus of the counsel, she said, was keeping the family together. "My husband was finally voted off the church board because he has a lady friend on the side, besides being abusive to me," she said. Adultery rather than years of abusiveness toward his wife prompted the church board to take disciplinary action against her husband.

Almost without exception women report that their pastors focused on getting them—not their abusive husbands—to change. Comments by pastors in our sample confirmed that stance. One minister said that his approach with abused women is to involve them in Bible studies because "the studies take their mind out of the home situation for a while," implying that his goal is to keep the wife preoccupied rather than to work for change. What this technique communicates to the battered woman is that the responsibility for change is hers; it becomes a spiritual strategy for blaming the victim.

"All three pastors said a man was 'head of the family' and I must endure whatever he did," one woman wrote. "My current pastor, after observing my husband's violence and anger, advised divorce but gave no more counseling or emotional support. He does not want to be perceived as an advocate of divorce." Since filing for divorce, that woman added, only two older women in her church talk to her. "I'm the outcast, being a victim of 'church discipline' for divorce, although my husband's behavior is well known."

Another woman was counseled by her pastor to go home and have sexual intercourse with her husband, who had just pointed a gun at her during an argument. The implication was, she said, that the more she gave herself to him, the more her abusive husband would respond in love and change his behavior. When that didn't work and his behavior became increasingly violent, she left him—and the church.

Tragically, that woman is not alone among abused women, many of whom have felt that leaving an abusive spouse also means leaving the church. One woman said she is "totally disillusioned" with the church after being told she was in the wrong for wanting to leave her abusive husband. "So for eighteen months I carried around a piece of paper with a Bible verse on it and acted as though my husband were 'Jesus' (that is, 'What would you do if this were Jesus living in your home?'). That was the main counseling I was given," she recalled bitterly. "I almost committed suicide that year."

Her comments are echoed by a plethora of Christian women who have been abused by their husbands and then abandoned by their churches when their marital problems became public. "Divorce is a stench in the nostrils of the church," a woman from the Southeast observed. Though her pastor advised against it, she divorced her husband after putting up with ten years of abuse. "I finally decided I didn't have to answer to the ministers, but to God," she concluded. "It was my neck being squeezed, not theirs."

Surely all women are born knowing the men they love could kill them in a minute, that we are kept alive by kindness, that we are always in peril. This is the source of our desire for obedience, for the inherited knack, the alert readiness—even in women who rage or live their lives in solitude—for giving in.

Mary Gordon[1]

_____

2
Who Is the Battered Woman, and Why Does She Stay?

She comes from every class, every ethnic group, every walk of life. She sits in the church pew next to you each week. She's that woman across the street, the schoolteacher, attorney, waitress. She may be one of the office secretaries, perhaps the minister's wife. She even may be your daughter. If current research is correct, roughly every other married woman you meet will at some point in her marriage experience at least one incident of physical violence at the hands of her husband.[2]

While the precise number of women who experience at least one incident of physical violence inflicted by their husbands cannot be determined, several studies suggest that fifty per cent is a reliable, perhaps even conservative, estimate. A 1988 estimate by the National

Coalition against Domestic Violence suggests that three to four million women are beaten annually in their homes by husbands, ex-husbands or lovers. Those figures account only for severe physical assaults which receive police and medical attention.[3]

"Violence against wives is a crime of enormous proportions," contend authors Carolyn and Jim Barden in *The Battered Wife Syndrome,* noting that "it occurs in families from all racial, economic, educational, and religious backgrounds."[4] While low-income battered women are more visible because they seek help from public agencies, middle- and upper-class women are also victimized but often go to hotels and private agencies for refuge.

A front-page *Wall Street Journal* article on February 25, 1985, reported that John Fedders, director of enforcement for the Securities and Exchange Commission, had confessed in a public divorce trial to periodically beating his wife. "The Fedders marriage is a textbook example of a phenomenon that social and medical workers say affects millions of other American families," the article contends. "And despite a common notion that wife-beating prevails mostly among blue-collar workers, it is no less common among the white-collar classes and the professional elite."[5]

In a letter to her husband telling him she wanted a divorce, Charlotte Fedders wrote:

Can you possibly remember how many times you have beaten me? Why didn't you believe me when I said I would never let you do that to me again? Know this—no woman deserves to be beaten by her husband, not ever. . . . I can no longer have you living in the same house as the boys and me. . . . It is a shame because most men would kill to have children as good as yours to nurture, guide, and love. . . . And I would caution you not to be too macho in telling all your acquaintances about our situation—the truth will come out and no one admires a wife beater.[6]

Statistics on the extent of wife abuse vary depending on the severity of abuse being assessed, but author Maria Roy estimates that violence against wives occurs at least once in two-thirds of all marriages, while researchers Straus, Gelles and Steinmetz contend that about one-third of all wives are beaten during the course of their marriages.[7]

What constitutes physical abuse? Hitting, shoving, pinching, pulling, bruising, biting, kicking, scratching, stabbing, shooting, raping, slapping. A violent act is one that is "carried out with the knowledge that the likely consequences of it will be physical injury or pain to another person."[8]

In 1983 *Time* magazine outlined the "silent crime" of wife beating in a special section of articles devoted to domestic violence. The report looked at what has always existed:

> Nearly 6 million wives will be abused by their husbands in any one year. Some 2,000 to 4,000 women are beaten to death annually. The nation's police spend one-third of their time responding to domestic violence calls. Battery is the single major cause of injury to women, more significant than accidents, rapes or muggings.[9]

Gender and Violence

Despite the evidence that marital violence is mutual—wives acting violently toward their husbands, as well as husbands toward their wives—the severity of violence between husbands and wives varies greatly. Research indicates that when the severity and extent of injuries due to "husband battering" are examined, the assaults on men are statistically "insignificant and incomparable to those sustained by women."[10]

In his book *The Domestic Assault of Women,* psychologist Donald G. Dutton considers the issue of gender and the use of violence. He cites one national survey that found that when less-violent actions are considered, "more mutual use of violence is reported."[11] Dutton cautions that when assaultive incidents "are classified by injurious effects rather than use of violence, women are the victims 94% of the time."

Thus he concludes that the effects of male violence "are far more serious than those of female violence."[12] In any event, "husband assault is not a major social problem because few males are injured by female violence." Wife assault, "on the other hand, does produce serious injuries and physical risk."[13]

Psychiatrist Daniel Saunders found that increases in "minor violence" by wives were associated with "sharp increases in the number of severe assaults by their partners." Women who behaved violently toward their spouse reported that "self-defense was the most common motive for both nonsevere and severe violence." Only a few women indicated using violence that was "likely to cause serious injuries."[14]

Sociologist Murray Straus reports that husbands are much more severe in their displays of violence than their wives, with the average number of "severely violent assaults by husbands on nonviolent wives . . . three times greater than the number of severe assaults by wives on nonviolent husbands. . . . Outside the family, the cultural norm which makes hitting a woman more taboo than hitting a man prevails—but not so inside the family. Men who would not dream of hitting a woman, hit their wives."[15]

One consequence of this high rate of violence against women, concludes Straus, is that women themselves become more violent.

> Victimization tends to train people to victimize others. Being a victim of violence does not turn one against violence. On the contrary, it tends to be a powerful pro-violence learning experience. . . . Therefore, the more a wife is assaulted by her husband, the more likely she is to incorporate violence in her own behavioral repertory.[16]

The "Victim-Prone" Personality

Are there specific personality traits of a "victim-prone personality for the woman"? No, says psychologist Lenore Walker, one of the foremost authorities in wife abuse research. Most of the women she interviewed

in a three-year study were "intelligent, well-educated, competent people who held responsible jobs," and they "appeared" to be similar to
other people. She notes, however, that this appearance was mostly
maintained at "great psychological cost." Battered women "develop a
positive sense of self from having survived a violent relationship which
causes them to believe they are equal or better than others," Walker
asserts.[17]

From her work with battered wives, therapist Carol Victor concludes
that the abusive marriage fulfills needs for the woman which often
stem from unhealthy childhood influences:

The battered wife is not blameless. Whatever is happening, it is
satisfying some unhealthy need that should be clarified—perhaps
a need from childhood to believe that she cannot do much of anything, or that she needs to be kept under control. At the thought
of removing herself from the violent marriage, she thinks, "I know
what I've got; I'm scared of what I might get!" Why is she comfort-
able with this behavior? It's part of the battered personality. It's
what she's been subjected to all her life.[18]

In the Christian Home

We Christians like to hope that wife abuse in our homes is not as
prevalent as it is in society at large, but there is little data with which
to make estimates. In a 1974 study of eighty families, sociologist
Richard Gelles found more nonreligious than religious homes involved
in expressions of violence. For those families in which the husband
had no religious involvement, violence was more frequent, occurring
on a daily to monthly basis. Gelles concluded that there was "a generally high level of violence in families when one or both of the spouses
is an agnostic, atheist, or has no religion."[19] While violence levels were
not appreciably different for families from various religious groups,
violence levels were noted to be higher for families in which the
spouses' denominational commitments differed (a Catholic married to

a Lutheran, for instance).

Lenore Walker, whom we quoted earlier, in her book *The Battered Woman,* calls it a myth to think that religious beliefs will prevent battering. Walker notes that the religious women in her study "all indicated that their religious beliefs did not protect them from their assaultive men."[20] Similarly, after studying abused women at a Los Angeles area shelter, Barbara Star concluded that a religious upbringing "encourages traditional and conservative role behavior and discourages marital dissolution, which may heighten a woman's susceptibility to being victimized."[21]

The majority of the women Walker interviewed grew up in what she calls "religious" homes, and she found that their beliefs and values primarily served to maintain the family unit. While most of the women in her study reported religious beliefs and some felt that their belief in a deity "helped them endure their suffering, offering comfort and solace," others abandoned their faith because it created conflict with the batterer or because of unsuccessfully seeking "help from a religious or spiritual leader."[22]

The groups most adamant about denying help to battered women were

the conservative fundamentalists and some orders of Catholicism. While they might assist the woman during a crisis period, they would send her home to "preserve the family" when the need for immediate safety passed, advice which accompanied being instructed by their religious adviser to go home, pray for the batterer's soul, and hope that he would become a better person.[23]

Walker's findings are supported by other researchers who assert that the counseling pastor often confirms the traditional mindset which fostered the abuse or ignores the abusive experience.

While religious faith can be very significant for the abused woman, the subject has received limited attention in the Christian community. In 1981 the United Methodist General Board of Global Ministries conducted a study of 600 Methodist women, perhaps the first study designed to examine wife abuse in the Christian home. The results showed that "one out of every six women reported abuse by their husbands" and for one-fourth of those "the abusive treatment involved physical battering."[24]

One study alone cannot be considered an authoritative analysis of the problem in Christian homes. However, one can conservatively estimate that for every sixty married women in a church, ten suffer emotional and verbal abuse, and two or three will be physically abused by their husbands. What is perhaps more disturbing is that the majority of the women did not tell anyone within their church about the abuse, and "if they did eventually seek help, it was most often from outside the church."

Why Does a Woman Stay?

One of the first questions asked by those who have never known abuse is, "Why does a woman stay in an abusive relationship?" That question is often accompanied by the boast, "If anyone ever laid a hand on me, I'd be out the door in a second!"

There is no clear-cut answer why a woman remains in an abusive relationship since the "why" consists of a web of interrelated factors—emotional, legal, religious, psychological, economic, familial. The more responsible question to ask, then, is not "Why does she stay" but "What in our community is keeping her there?"

Rather than initiate divorce, a professional woman from Texas endured twelve years of violence, only then to have her husband leave her to marry another woman. The man, once a church deacon, raped her before their marriage, strangled, kicked and bruised her (in one instance bruises were documented on over sixty per cent of her body) and repeatedly threatened murder. Why did she stay? "He threatened to kill the children and make me watch if I left him," she said. "And with one infant and a four-year-old I had no place to go. I left after one beating and walked around town trying to get help, but I thought no one would help me or believe me because he had just been nominated 'Man of the Year.' He ridiculed me and beat me when I returned home."

Out of guilt, fear, a sense of religious duty, helplessness or just a lack of options, battered women generally stay with their abusive husbands long after it is safe or reasonable to assume that change will come. Most battered women do not attempt to gain their freedom from a battering relationship, says Walker, because "they do not believe they can gain escape from the batterer's domination."[25]

They are often right. News reports abound of situations similar to that of the Minnesota woman whose ex-husband returned after twenty-six years and held her at gunpoint until she was able to calm him down. Six weeks later the man broke into her home and shot her four times before a neighbor intervened. Said the county sheriff, "A lot of women and children live in terror of this kind of domestic situation. We sit on the edge of our seats waiting for something to happen."[26]

Dr. Constance Doran, founding director of Fuller Theological Seminary's SAFE (Stop Abusive Family Environments) Program, distinguishes between "external sociological" reasons for staying in a battering relationship and "internal psychological" motivations. She cites ignorance of one's legal rights or economic dependence on the abusive husband as examples of the former and an "internal paralysis" as an example of the latter.

It's very much like what victims of political terrorism experience: a psychological numbing process goes on, so that the person is able to tolerate the violent situation as well as possible. Victims tend to minimize the risk they are experiencing. An extension of this may occur when the victim actually becomes a supporter or advocate of her captor. After the person is free, often she participates in defending the captor. The whole process of becoming psychologically paralyzed is significant in keeping women in abusive situations.[27]

Women also stay in abusive relationships, Doran contends, because "our culture has trained women to be relatively forgiving and passive in the face of threat. From early childhood women are taught not to respond aggressively when threatened."

Similarly, psychologist Steve Morgan has coined the term "conjugal terrorism" to describe the coercive control present in wife abuse in which the attitudes and behavior of the violent husband resemble those of the political terrorist. "Conjugal terrorism is the use or threatened use of violence in order to break down the resistance of the victim to the will of the terrorist."[28]

In their study of marital dependency and wife abuse, researchers Debra Kalmuss and Murray Straus determined that it is "economic and not psychological dependency which keeps women in severely abusive marriages." They conclude that "dependent wives have fewer alternatives to marriage and fewer resources within marriage with which to negotiate changes in their husbands' behavior. Thus, marital dependency reinforces the likelihood that women will tolerate physical abuse from their husbands."[29]

Some women report a new sense of freedom when they obtain knowledge about their legal rights. They are reminded they may come and go as they please. According to the law, their homes do not belong exclusively to their husbands. Abused women can gain new confidence when they realize they have potential leverage against their abusive spouses.

The Victim as Missionary

Of the many battered women Constance Doran has counseled, the majority are "warm, intelligent women, very nurturing, empathetic and often devout Christians" who see themselves entirely responsible for their husbands' emotional and spiritual well-being. Doran contends that these women have "rescue fantasies of saving their mate from violent impulses, much as a missionary may dream of converting a savage tribe." Those fantasies motivate them to repeatedly endure their husbands' violence. Such women are caregivers who interpret violent acts as evidence that their husbands need their help.

"She takes pleasure in her dream of being his rescuer," Doran noted. "Her ability to endure his violence is not seen as helplessness or masochism, but rather as evidence of her moral strength. She is the nurturing mother, he is the naughty child whose violence is merely another sign of his immaturity and consequently his need for her."

Out of the twenty-one domestic violence cases Doran handled during one two-year period, she saw this missionary syndrome at work in seventeen of the situations. "It keeps women locked into an abusive relationship," Doran said. "They feel that if they just hang in there long enough and turn the other cheek one more time, then he will change. And women are particularly encouraged to do this in the Christian community."

Reports we have received from battered women certainly bolster Doran's findings. Seventy per cent of our sample of nearly one hundred women agreed that it was their responsibility to save their husbands from themselves. A Florida woman, still married to an abusive Christian man, said: "I don't think physical abuse is any worse than what the disciples went through. There's a lot of torment in the Psalms; Job went through a lot. My reward will be in heaven. If I stand faithful, my children will follow me." But she was troubled by the fact that her young son already mirrors his father's abusive actions. "I hope it's normal," she said.

A woman from the Midwest said that when she survived an attempted strangling early in her marriage, she thought, " 'I'm incredible. If I can make it through this, I can make it through anything.' My parents told me to see what I could do to change; they had no concern for my safety. I felt betrayed, but I started believing it. I felt called to be a missionary to my husband, to the child I had married." Finally seeking a divorce after twenty-nine years of marriage, she wants younger women to know that they shouldn't put up with such treatment. "I was going to school, I was a wife, I was a mother. I even did workshops for churches on how to handle problems. I could deceive myself and let everyone know that this was my calling and it was a joy."

But when she became seriously ill, her whole life changed. "I had to start taking care of myself. I couldn't be Supermom and Superwife. Here was this indispensable missionary—how could I get sick? But it was a relief to disengage from that role. When I finally said to myself, 'I am crazy. I have been a fool to live this way,' it was a relief."

An Accomplice to Her Own Battering

In her examination of why women stay in abusive relationships, Lenore Walker has proposed a three-phase "cycle theory" of wife battering. During phase one, the wife blames herself for her husband's explosion. Such a perception encourages her to feel she deserved the beating that followed and must accept her aggressor's justification.

"When he throws the dinner she prepared for him across the kitchen floor, she reasons that maybe she did overcook it, accidently," Walker says. "As she cleans up his mess, she may think that he was a bit extreme in his reaction, but she is usually so grateful that it was a relatively minor incident that she resolves not to be angry with him. Perhaps he had trouble at work or . . . This reasoning unfortunately does not bring an improvement." The accumulated effects of this phase on the victim vary from an increase in the level of her anger to a rigid denial of the problem.

The second phase of the battering process—the actual violence—involves an accumulating rage on the part of the husband that is often so overwhelming and frightening for the woman (particularly if she has experienced a history of battering) that she may respond by stimulating the confrontation. The presence of fear and threat can be so great that as a result of previous exposure the abused woman will intentionally short-circuit the mounting tension, quickly get the violence over with and try to alleviate her fear.

Lest one rashly assume that battered women in general derive some sort of masochistic joy from their abuse, this phenomenon of "baiting" the husband must be examined in the context of the entire cycle of battering.[30] Although frightening and painful, the actual violence is generally less terrifying than living in a constant state of uncertainty and threat. Thus, wives often admit having provoked their husbands in order to move through the abuse.

The result is a gripping sense of guilt which locks victims into an even more destructive process of self-blaming. This phase leaves the woman so paralyzed by fear, terror and dread that, after the violence, she will deny her need for medical attention to avoid fully realizing her predicament.

Phase three, Walker suggests, is a time of mutual pleasantness in which the batterer is contrite, placating and obsessed with concern for his mate. The abused wife often overestimates the validity of such change and, because she badly wants to believe her pain is ended, convinces herself that all will be well in the future. "The traditional notion that two people who love each other will overcome all kinds of odds against them prevails," Walker notes. "The battered woman chooses to believe that the behavior she sees during phase three signifies what her man is really like."[31]

Walker's 1983 investigation of 403 self-identified battered women again confirmed the existence of this cycle of battering. But, she noted, "over time, the first phase of tension building becomes more common and loving contrition, or the third phase, declines."[32] As Walker conceptualizes it, then, this cycle of violence typically finds the woman abandoning her emotional and physical safety by denying what is really occurring. She instead accepts an illusive hope that her husband's contrite behavior indicates how he will behave in the future. Ultimately, however, this translucent dream only increases a woman's personal sense of embarrassment and self-rejection as she copes with the fact that "she is selling herself for the few moments of phase-three loving." In this way, Walker suggests, the woman becomes "an accomplice to her own battering."

Violence is a way of proving that one exists, when one believes oneself to be insignificant.

Paul Tournier[1]

3
What Kind of Men Abuse Their Wives?

fter beating his wife, the minister bound her to the bed with a dog chain. Three days later he loosened the chain a couple of notches because his wife's hands were getting numb. When the pastor finally left his battered wife alone, she escaped.

This chilling illustration is true. But what revealed that man's warped world view, even more than the dehumanizing abuse to which he had subjected his wife, was his incredulous response after the court mandated that he participate in a program for abusers. "Here I was being kind to her by loosening the chain," he charged, "and she took advantage of it."

What kind of person could treat a fellow human being with such cruelty? The answer, say some, lies in the fact that the minister in question learned unacceptable methods of coping with anger and stress—methods that can be unlearned and replaced with more productive behavior.

No Friends

Some experts blame violence toward women on the "emotional illiteracy" of men who have been taught to keep a stiff upper lip and show no emotion. They are those of whom a *Washington Post* columnist wrote, "My friends have no friends. The reason for that is that we are all men—and men, I have come to believe, cannot or will not have real friends. They have something else—companions, buddies, pals, chums, someone to drink with and someone to wench with and someone to lunch with, but no one when it comes to saying how they feel— especially how they hurt."[2] Men who have no outlet for ordinary, everyday anger are at risk of finally exploding in rage toward the people who have to put up with it: their wives.

Christian psychologist Constance Doran characterizes the abusive man as one who is often very dependent, possessive and deferential. Roughly sixty per cent of the abusers with whom she worked were themselves abused or saw their fathers abusing their mothers. "Typically the violence pattern begins with the wife's first pregnancy and is really directed toward the fetus," Doran said. "There's going to be another sibling and the husband is jealous. He wants and needs nurturing and at the same time hates it." The more saintlike and forgiving the wife is, the more it puts the husband in a victim role, and he doesn't like it. Often pastors and counselors play right into the problem by asking a woman, "What did you do to cause his violence?"

Rather than learning techniques for being more sensitive to her husband's desires, the wife needs to let her husband bear the consequences for his violence, Doran contends.

The first step is to let the husband grow up and take responsibility for controlling his impulses. He needs to experience the natural consequences of his behavior.

By her compliance, the wife reinforces his violence. She exerts tremendous levels of energy to meet his every need. He hits her. The neighbors call the police. She says she fell and doesn't press charges. By lying and covering up for her husband, the wife provides negative reinforcement for his violence. She is reinforcing tantrum behavior in a man who on the exterior may be very macho, but inside is as possessive as a two-year-old.[3]

Such was the case of Todd.[4] He described himself as "alternately affectionate and distant, interested and apathetic, loving and cold." Caught between a negative self-image and a fear of intimacy, Todd said he used violence and the threat of violence as a means of controlling his wife's behavior, "so that she wouldn't do or say anything that might serve to remind me that I just might have a few problems." By beating his wife for one of her real or imagined faults, he could avoid facing his own sense of inadequacy.

"I was and had always been absolutely dependent on women," Todd said. "I went to women for my validation as a man and for recognition of my personal value, to gain courage, to obtain forgiveness, to seek advice and to heal my pain. Those are tremendous responsibilities to lay on anyone, and whenever these needs couldn't be filled, I felt betrayed and angry. This excessive dependence also caused me a lot of fear. . . . In my usual manner of dealing with negative emotion, I immediately transformed these fears into anger."

Because of his dependency Todd was overwhelmed by the pressure of culturally determined sex roles that say "men are supposed to be strong, brave, independent and self-sufficient." So he learned to treat women as little girls—"but little girls who were totally responsible for my happiness or lack of it." One way he would try to foster the illusion of independence, Todd noted, was "to relegate any woman on whom I was dependent to an inferior status, to deny them the right to determine the nature of our relationship, to try to force them to believe that they were actually dependent on me. . . . My wife thought that by being whatever I wanted her to be, she would please me, which she did, but her success at it also frightened me terribly. She wound up being beaten for doing exactly what I wanted her to do."

Dual Personalities

Abuse expert Lenore Walker describes the typical batterer as someone with a dual personality. He is both charming and cruel, selfish and generous, extraordinarily possessive and extremely jealous, and a man whose greatest fear is that his woman will leave him.[5]

The batterer often has a history from childhood of responding to frustration and emotional distress in angry and violent ways such as being violent toward pets, inanimate objects or other people. Added to this, says Walker, is a "history of temper tantrums, insecurity, a need to keep the environment stable and nonthreatening, jealousy and possessiveness. The man's ability to be charming, manipulative and seductive to get what he wants, and hostile, nasty and mean when he does not succeed, makes the risk for battering very high."[6]

Abusers are often suspicious and jealous, suffer from low self-esteem and need to assert themselves. Generally, they are intolerant of their wives functioning in a superior position. Nevertheless, research shows that men who batter are generally of normal mental health.[7] Richard Gelles summarizes the role of psychopathology in the scenario of wife abuse:

> After ten years of continued research and administration of countless psychological tests, the summary evaluation of the psychopathological approach to domestic violence is that the proportion of individuals who batter . . . and suffer from psychological disorders is no greater than the proportion of the population in general with psychological disorders.[8]

In a general sense, the personality structure of the batterer typifies that of many men within our culture.

Alcohol and Abuse

Christy Telch and Carol Linquist, in their 1984 study of 100 subjects, found that while alcohol use was the best predictor of membership in the violent-couple sample, alcohol did not necessarily cause the battering. "It is possible," they contend, "that the temporary control or calm established after a violent episode reinforces violence, much as alcohol provides temporary escape from other problems."[9]

Such a perspective is consistent with the research findings of Berk and others who gathered data from 262 domestic-disturbance incidents in which police intervened. In examining how alcohol abuse affected the violence between couples, they concluded that whatever the disinhibiting impact of alcohol, "it does not seem to trigger more serious incidents." They suggest instead that "unhappy" men can become both problem drinkers and be more active in abusing their wives, but "drinking is not an immediate and direct cause of those injuries."[10]

Of the nearly 100 Christian women we interviewed or polled, eighteen per cent identified their husbands as having a serious drinking problem. While some stated that their husbands were only abusive when drinking, a greater number felt that the men drank because they were "just miserable" or because it gave them an excuse to be violent. Few of the women blamed their husbands' violence on the drinking; most felt that it was only part of a larger process.

As one former abuser and recovering alcoholic stated: "Drinking was like pouring gasoline on smouldering coals." The unresolved anger and abusive tendencies were there, he said, and using alcohol helped ignite an explosion that was bound to occur. Another abuser noted that "although many batterers are chemically dependent, most are not, and battering is *not* a symptom of alcoholism which will magically disappear if only the poor guy could sober up. Both the development of my alcoholism and my use of violence to control my personal relationships were associated with problems in my personality and with my feelings about myself and my environment."[11]

Master Manipulator

For several years former pastor Dan Keller has been supervising therapy groups for batterers, offered by the Indianapolis Salvation Army. Four 26-week groups are run simultaneously and are always filled to capacity. Referrals come primarily through the courts.

Labelling wife abusers as "master manipulators," Keller says he works at getting them "narrowly focused so they don't get off on sidetracks. For the first ten to fifteen weeks I don't believe anything they say."[12] Keller's confrontational approach starts by breaking behavior down into small parts. "When you do that it gets extremely uncomfortable for the abuser. I don't look at the big picture—what she did to justify his behavior. I don't care what your wife did. In my group it isn't important. It's what you did, how you responded."

Keller's first goal with an abuser is to get him to "own up to the fact that he is abusive." Gradually he helps abusers examine their emotions. "They think anger is the only emotion they have. We look at how they feel, how their bodies are feeling." Yet abusiveness, says Keller, is a learned behavior. "With the exception of an occasional miracle, most of the time in the Christian relationship anything we learn we have to unlearn, as Paul said, by the renewing of the mind. The process of unlearning and relearning new behaviors is a process of lifestyle."

Keller doesn't introduce the Christian perspective until the end of the program because "most abusers have gotten saved, baptized or had some religious experience before coming to see me as another way to manipulate their wives. If they know I'm an ordained minister, then they want to refocus their problem in terms of my theological position."

Though he has seen the effectiveness of the Indianapolis program for abusers of all types—"I've had ministers in my group, and those from derelicts to Ph.D.'s, men of all socioeconomic and intelligence levels"—Keller is cautious about making predictions about the success of the program in terms of reconciliation. "When abusiveness has gone on for ten to fifteen years, the memories of those problems for the victim will hinder reconciliation for years. It depends how you define reconciliation."

From his experience, Keller postulates that wife abuse in Christian homes is a tremendous problem. "My work would lead me to believe that the more fundamental a church is, the higher the probability that abuse is happening. While the Bible admonishes a woman to be subject to her husband, there is no place that even hints that the husband is to be dominant over the wife. I'm not sure what 'man as the head of the house' means, but a lot of abusers are. I find no basis for the chain of command in Scripture."

Between eighty and eighty-five per cent of the abusers who go through the Indianapolis program either were abused as children or saw their mothers abused. "If you wash away all the issues, these men are as much victims as anyone. Many of the same symptoms we see in the wife from being a victim we see in the abuser because his life has reinforced certain behaviors."

Traditional therapeutic approaches are ineffective with abusers, claims Keller, because you "counsel to the pain, you focus on her. The minute you do that you reinforce him.

"As hard as I push these fellows and despite all the baloney they give me, no one says, 'You don't understand.' I'm the one person who won't let them do what they do to everyone else. I'm the one person who refuses, without manipulating them, to be manipulated by them."

Offering Hope

In Quincy, Illinois, Paul Hegstrom's approach for dealing with abusers is equally confrontational.[13] Based on the assumption that men deny feelings, the treatment program Hegstrom has developed offers hope to abusers.

"I've never seen a bad man walk through these doors," claims Hegstrom. "We teach them what reality and normalcy really are. These are men who have never been taught how to love." With Hosea 4:6—"My people are destroyed from lack of knowledge"—as a guide, Hegstrom has developed a program of behavior modification through education. Abusers meet twice a week for group therapy to trace their anger to its roots and to be retrained in how to love.

A pastor and former abuser, Hegstrom established his first Domestic Violence Learning Center in 1985 after completing an eleven-month program for abusers and remarrying the woman he had battered for years. Within three years, six satellite centers had opened across the country, and 120 people were being serviced each month in the Quincy center alone.

Raised in a minister's home, Hegstrom says he went through "forty years of rebellion against everything." He pinpoints the origin of his anger to abandonment as a child and experiences of child molestation. Because of Hegstrom's anger, his family was placed "in a lose-lose situation."

Hegstrom acknowledges that as an abuser he knew he was doing something wrong. "I had so many unresolved conflicts in my own life and I had no tools," he said. "Anger was my feeling and there was nothing under it. I had no knowledge of any type of feeling. Anger and control were it for me."

Though he has done no formal therapeutic-outcome research, Hegstrom claims a restoration rate of eight out of ten marriages. "Men will wade through hell for hope," he noted.

Treating the Batterer

In a study of forty-four of the eighty programs across the country for batterers, researcher Albert Roberts found that the social-learning theory of aggression was the main theory used. "This framework postulates that because violence is a learned behavior, people are capable of changing their behavior and learning nonviolent methods of coping with anger and stress."[14] The focus of these programs is on educating abusers about battering and anger control.

In *Counseling for Family Violence and Abuse*, Christian psychologist Grant Martin outlines principles of treatment for batterers, beginning with the assumption that "abusive anger is a learned behavior." He, however, sees it as stemming "out of the basic nature of humankind."[15] While such behavior may start small, Martin believes, it will eventually contaminate the entire relationship.

> Abusive behavior starts in the heart of one person, but eventually the whole system is defiled. Within a violent relationship, the abuser becomes more skilled at violence and the wife becomes more skilled at being a victim. . . . The agenda becomes one of identifying the cues, prompts, or button-pushing events that lead to violence.[16]

The relational problems that exist in an abusive marriage—low self-esteem, poor problem-solving and conflict-resolution skills, for instance—must not be the initial focus of therapy, warns Martin.

> It's too dangerous to discuss the problems of marriage until everyone is safe. Any problems with conflict resolution or communication cannot be realistically discussed while the husband is blatantly abusing power. Trust and confidence cannot be developed unless safety is achieved.[17]

If emergency services for victims have only recently been implemented, treatment programs for abusers have been even longer in coming. Evaluating the successfulness of such programs is difficult because of variations in how "success" is defined and variations in the length of time for which behavior change is monitored. One group leader noted that while he was fairly confident that the majority of batterers who complete his program stop their physical abuse, he could not accurately predict what percentage would rechannel their anger into other forms of abuse (emotional, sexual, child).

A program in Ann Arbor, Michigan, found violence diminished in eighty-seven per cent of its cases within one year of operation.[18] And a survey of leaders of treatment groups for batterers determined that for every 100 men enrolled, sixty completed the program. Of those sixty, forty-two to fifty-three do not return to battering within a year.[19] These percentages, however, were "based on educated estimates" rather than systematic research. Furthermore, because no controls existed we do not know what percentage of those men would have stopped battering without treatment. In his assessment of the research in this area, psychologist Donald Dutton concludes that thirty-three per cent of those treated "would be expected not to repeat assault even without treatment."[20]

In Albert Roberts's nationwide survey of programs for batterers, he found that seventy per cent of the programs evaluated cited "a lack of motivation and commitment among the men" as the greatest roadblock to success.[21] "Battering can be likened to an addiction to alcohol," observed Roberts. "An alcoholic may be able to stay away from liquor for a lengthy period, but must always be on guard against a set of circumstances which would trigger a return to the bottle."[22]

Rescue me, O LORD, from evil men; protect me from men of violence,
who devise evil plans in their hearts and
stir up war every day. They make their tongues as sharp as a serpent's;
the poison of vipers is on their lips.
Keep me, O LORD, from the hands of the wicked; protect me from men of
violence who plan to trip my feet.

Psalm 140:1-4

4
Evil:
The Heart of
Violence

'*ve lived my whole life feeling like I wasn't okay,*" he said
matter-of-factly. "As a kid I was beat by my dad, strung up with
hoses and chains. When Dad was drunk he'd get me and my six
brothers and sisters out of bed and beat us up. If anything was
wrong he'd beat us all, sometimes three or four times a day.
Once when he attempted to kill everyone, we ran to the neighbors
naked in minus 20 degrees to save ourselves." Kurt was a Bible-college
student and a wife beater. He'd been a Christian for four years and
married for six. His childhood was a story of conflict, pain, rejection,
violence. These patterns carried over into his marriage.

"My grandfather was murdered and thrown into the Tennessee Riv-
er, so my dad never had anyone to discipline him. Many times when

Dad was drunk and beating us, he'd say, 'You kids should be thankful you have someone to teach you right from wrong.'

"When I finally sat in a group of batterers, within forty-five minutes I knew I was an abuser. I saw how low I really was. One of the men was a murderer. The demographics were identical to mine. The only thing that separated me from him was time."

But now Kurt was trying to shrug off the weight of his grim past and start over. He desperately wanted to save his fragile marriage, and yet he felt stymied, overpowered and destined to fail.

"I feel like Satan is almost everywhere when I'm alone," he admitted. "I get very afraid and I feel the presence of evil around me, like something is trying to hurt me. I feel like I have a problem that will keep me from ever being close to another human being."

The Reality of Evil

Evil exists. And because, as historian Jeffrey Burton Russell says, it is "real, absolute and tangible," it demands our consideration. "We avoid examining it at our grave peril," he cautions. Identifying violence as the "heart of evil," Russell believes that Satan dwells in "the evil infliction of suffering."

Social scientists who study domestic violence and daily witness such evil do not seriously consider evil as a factor in family violence. Most, in fact, would dismiss evil as an outdated superstition.

Rex J. Beaber, a UCLA professor of family medicine hired to interview death-row murderers and provide expert testimony to the court, says that hours of terrifying tales have forced him to ask, Is there evil? "Could there be an extra force, a dark force, that works through humans and perpetrates terror? Certainly my subjects appear possessed when they act out their visions of carnage. Might they literally be possessed? Are they evil, or does an evil force temporarily inhabit their soul? To take such questions seriously is a sin in my profession."[1]

Treatment programs that are founded on the fallacy that violence is due purely to poor thinking, wrong choices or a lack of personal awareness focus almost exclusively on retraining abusers. They emphasize the need for the abuser to know his feelings, identify his inner frustrations and redirect his responses. Such an approach, though useful, is limited: it fails to recognize the ultimate source of the violence. The kind of change that must occur if violence is to be eradicated—a change of heart—never transpires. And if evil is said *not* to exist, only personal preferences are left to decide moral behavior. There are no unchanging standards of what is good and evil.

When violence is seen only on a material level, as something which can be analyzed, identified or systematized on a flow chart, there is no need to consider the spiritual. But it is precisely within the spiritual realm that evil must first be confronted.

Most battered women have no trouble accepting the fact that evil exists and that their raging husbands at times have literally become Satan's henchmen. One Minneapolis woman told us: "If he didn't abuse me physically, he might rave all night. He would run me down, shouting and cursing. He would talk so filthy and foam at the mouth. It was like speaking in tongues from Satan." And a woman from Florida, who checked her husband's hands for knives before getting into bed with him, said she was "the mirror of what my husband didn't want to see. My husband would say things like, 'You're so straight I can't stand it. I walk into this house and feel God staring at me.' He'd get very angry, and it would come out at me."

A California woman labeled her unbelieving husband "possessed."

I can see it by the things that take place. It's so evident. The Lord and Satan. I can see both sides. He's gotten worse and worse. He hasn't spoken to me since the baby was born ten months ago, unless it is filthy, disgusting language in front of the kids. I see the evil and disgusting things he's done. Even with the kids, wanting to show them things on the video recorder. I've really seen spiritual battles.

The Lust for Power

The violence of the batterer is violence on one's own behalf. It is violence designed to serve oneself and attain power over others. It is violence based on a lust for power, a lust which destroys. This lust is an indulgence of "the desires of the flesh and of the mind" according to Paul. It reveals a commitment to "the ways of this world . . . to the ruler of the kingdom of the air, the spirit who is now at work in those who are disobedient" (Eph 2:2-3).

In Scripture, we discover that evil is not a mere abstraction; it is tangible, and violence is its handiwork. We are warned not to "walk in the way of evil men" for they "eat the bread of wickedness and drink the wine of violence" (Prov 4:14,17). And their violence is verbal as well. "Violence overwhelms the mouth of the wicked," Proverbs 10:6 tells us.

The psalmist prays for protection against the wickedness of the tongue. "Rescue me, O LORD, from evil men; protect me from men of violence, who devise evil plans in their hearts and stir up war every day. They make their tongues as sharp as a serpent's; the poison of vipers is on their lips" (Ps 140:1-3). For many battered women the unpredictable treachery of a deadly serpent is an apt characterization of the abusive actions of their husbands.

James warns us dramatically that the tongue is like a fire which consumes the whole person. "It is a restless evil, full of deadly poison" (Jas 3:8), and when permitted to have full license, it takes life into its own hand under the guidance of the evil one. "It corrupts the whole person, sets the whole course of his life on fire, and is itself set on fire by hell" (Jas 3:6).

While "damn you" and "go to hell" are rarely thought of as theological terms, such language does indicate a desire to act as judge over another's life. Physical violence is an example of this desire put into motion. It becomes a means of taking another person's life into one's hands, usurping the divine prerogative of judgment and misusing it.

Just as anger begets anger, so verbal abuse often signals the physical violence that is to come.

By its very definition, justice is to be meted out without anger and with impartiality. God is just and slow to anger; he alone can handle wrath. Satan comes to "kill and destroy," in direct opposition to God's creative purposes. And the verbal expression of violence is the starting point for becoming a slave to evil or giving the devil a foothold (Eph 4:27). It is also an expression of the condition of the heart. Jesus warned that the "things that come out of the mouth come from the heart, and these make a man 'unclean.' For out of the heart come evil thoughts, murder, adultery, sexual immorality, theft, false testimony, slander. . . . The evil man brings evil things out of the evil stored up in him" (Mt 15:18-19; 12:35).

Power Versus Authority

In his use of violence, the batterer is serving the cause of Satan in the world (see Jn 10:10). Violence is a means of asserting that one is powerful and is perceived by the abuser as a legitimate avenue for establishing power. Might which controls and appropriates solely for self fosters an appetite for even more power. Consequently, the pursuit of power actually enslaves the seeker to evil and can easily lead to moral, spiritual and physical death.

"Power and authority must not be confused," cautions Charles Colson. "Power is the ability to affect one's ends or purposes in the world. Authority is having not only the power (might), but the *right* to affect one's purpose. Power is often maintained by naked force; authority springs from a moral foundation."[2] While power is not inherently evil, it is "inherently corrupting," Colson asserts. Violence is a sign of the batterer's choice to allow such corruption to take root and become evil.

Losing One's Soul

The nature of evil is to seduce people into thinking that they have power when, in reality, the more they give in to evil the more deluded and controlled they become. They lose control of themselves. It is simply impossible to worship evil and still retain one's soul.

The abuser's violence is evidence of his belief that he can have power without personal destruction. Such is not the case. The batterer's delusion, that he can get others to serve his purposes by ruling in what he misconstrues as a godlike fashion, will result not in converts but in carnage. Ultimately the batterer is himself tricked by his lustful appetite, and his violent acts inevitably escalate. With each violent outburst the abuser testifies to the fact that he is a slave to the "modern idolatry of power."[3]

This type of destructive power is intimately linked to pride, states Richard Foster. "When pride is mixed with power the result is genuinely volatile. Pride makes us think we are right, and power gives us the ability to cram our vision of rightness down everyone else's throat. The marriage between pride and power carries us to the brink of the demonic."[4]

The Violence Within

Unfortunately, to accept the reality of evil in the destruction of marriages does not mean that we suddenly have a trouble-free tool with which to separate good from bad. The undeniable and disturbing fact is that violence exists within each of us. As evidence, Swiss physician Paul Tournier writes:

> Well-brought-up, reasonable, kindly people, gentle as lambs, can suddenly break out into brutal violence, in words, thoughts, or deeds—and it happens more often than you would imagine. The sheep suddenly turns into a wolf. I have on occasion slapped my wife, and I have often spoke to her in the most wounding terms. I might try to reassure myself with the thought that it was only a passing accident, a mental aberration, when I was no longer myself in the heat of the moment—something soon put right! It would be

more honest to say to myself that it was I who did it, and to see
that it reveals an aspect of myself that I find hard to recognize; that
I am much more violent than I care to acknowledge.[5]

We are all, as Tournier says, "contradictory beings," abhorring violence
and yet, at times, acting in violent ways. It is the contradictory nature
of humankind that makes the struggle with evil so complicated. It
would be different, as Aleksandr Solzhenitsyn notes, if there were "evil
people somewhere insidiously committing evil deeds, and it were necessary only to separate them from the rest of us and destroy them. But
the line dividing good and evil cuts through the heart of every human
being."[6] We have no grounds for flattery or self-deception; we cannot
view our own acts of violence, however minor, as legitimate.

To be disconnected from our own violent nature fosters a dangerous
attitude which sees the "truly nonviolent" person as separated from
the "truly violent" person by miles of conscience, compassion or emotional control. Yet it is only when we come face to face with our own
sinful natures, and thus our need of God's grace, that we can offer
grace to the violent abuser. "It is not a case of there being two camps,"
contends Tournier, "the camp of the violent and that of the nonviolent, however hard the latter try to hide their violence. But though
Jesus puts all men in the same camp, it is not in order to condemn
them all, but on the contrary to accord to all the divine grace."[7]

When we are honest, we come to the humbling realization that in
each abuser is a piece of us. Jesus recognized this when he stated that
anyone who was angry with his brother has committed murder in the
heart (Mt 5:22). Here Christ eradicates any subtle distinctions we
might make between degrees of violence as a way of defending our own
violent thoughts or actions. Jesus cuts through to the spawning
ground of violence: the human heart.

Thus, the fundamental issue of violence is not one of *actions* but
one of the condition of the heart. Until this heart condition is changed,
violence will continue its "dynamic of growth which condemns it to

increase."[8] Through Christ the bond of violence is broken and freedom from slavery realized. Jesus, as Tournier notes, "broke into the vicious circle of violence by taking upon himself the violence of men, and then refusing—though he knew how to be violent!—to pay back violence for violence."[9]

Crossing the Threshold

The recognition that good and evil are both active in each person's heart is no excuse for violent actions. As Solzhenitsyn rightly acknowledges, evildoing has a high threshold.

> Yes, a human being hesitates and bobs back and forth between good and evil all his life. He slips, falls back, clambers up, repents, things begin to darken again. But just so long as the threshold of evildoing is not crossed, the possibility of returning remains, and he himself is still within reach of our hope. But when, through the density of evil actions, the result either of their own extreme degree or of the absoluteness of his power, he suddenly crosses that threshold, he has left humanity behind, and without, perhaps, the possibility of return.[10]

At what point the abuser crosses that threshold we cannot say. It is not for us to decide when someone has given himself over to Satan, but the risk of becoming a slave to evil—once a journey down the path of violence has begun—is great. There is a process of engagement with evil that is evident in the lives of batterers, even among those who claim to have experienced rebirth in Christ.

Doing Battle with Evil

To believe in the existence of a personal Satan who perpetrates acts of violence and evil is not to dismiss the matter of personal responsibility. There are always human factors at play in any relationship. Clearly, people choose to act selfishly and in destructive ways despite the pain their actions will bring to others. And certainly not every action made without regard for the welfare of others can be labelled Satanic.

But when we perceive violence as primarily a response to stress, the result of poor family modeling or the outcome of a failure to be aware of one's feelings, we fail to accurately discern where the battle lies. Furthermore, we neutralize our ability to have any significant impact in the struggle. The reign of violence within many homes is evidence most basically of Satan's kingdom at work destroying order, love and happiness in human relationships. And until we enter the arena of domestic violence willing to battle evil, our efforts to see violence stopped and families transformed will be ineffective at best.

In his book *People of the Lie,* psychiatrist M. Scott Peck describes evil as "an opposition to life. It is that which opposes the life force. It has, in short, to do with killing." The killing, Peck continues, is "that which kills spirit"; it is that force "that seeks to kill life or liveliness." We need "to recognize evil for what it is, in all its ghastly reality," he states, and then must realize that evil is more often present in human relationships than usually acknowledged. "My own experience . . . is that evil human beings are quite common and usually appear quite ordinary to the superficial observer," Peck concludes.[11]

We cannot dismiss evil as some vague spiritual force that presides outside of human behavior. Evil is rooted in a superhuman personality: Satan. And when people are violent, hostile, argumentative, deceiving—accumulating, as it were, a treasure of evil goods within the economy of Satan—they gradually permit Satan to restructure their character and own them.

Whether using psychological or theological language, the truth remains that acts of evil are acts of sin. They are assaults on God's moral laws. They separate the evildoer from God and from fellow human beings. The result is that evil acts throw the individual into an abyss of aloneness. The destruction of a marriage, that earthly image of spiritual union with Christ and the most intimate of all human relationships, must certainly be a desired prize in the dominion of Satan.

The church's failure to effectively confront the problem of wife abuse, more than being just a reflection of a fundamental disregard for women or a fear of any challenge to a patriarchal system, is a reflection of the failure to recognize evil for what it is. Before Satan can be defeated, he must be identified. And, once identified, he must be fought on spiritual ground. The problem of wife abuse is not one of feminism, secular humanism or a lack of headship in the home. It is the problem of evil—unseen and unopposed.

When a wife explodes in an outburst of hysteria—an act of violence
which puts an end to a dialogue with her husband—it is a sign that the
dialogue has already failed, that she feels powerless to make
herself understood. It is she who is crossing the Rubicon, but it is her
husband who has made her cross it by his refusal to understand her.
The husband can flatter himself that he has remained calm and
apparently conciliatory; he has kept control of himself and can
blame his wife for her outburst.

Paul Tournier[1]

To claim that women provoke the violence of which they are so often
victims is to argue that Jewish passivity invited genocide or that the
exploited poor are to blame for the corruption of the rich.

Letty Cottin Pogrebin[2]

5
Blaming
the
Victim

would never in my wildest nightmares dream that my husband would ever abuse me, but he did. I took our two-month-old son and fled after the fourth time my husband struck me. My husband is a Christian, but his rage at things was unreal and it doesn't take much to end a human life when one is in an uncontrollable rage. I received counsel that it was my duty to stay and suffer for Jesus' sake. . . . I stayed with him then, misapplying Scriptures of how I was to act. I accepted what he did or didn't do and just tried to work on me, doing what was right."

"I was beaten and emotionally abused by my ex-husband. I left for six months, but when he saw a counselor and promised reform, I returned. I was not beaten after the return, but I found that my four-year-old daughter was—and sexually abused by him as well. The pastor I spoke to, the counselor I saw, the family doctor—all Christians—preferred to believe that I was lying, or at least to blame for the trouble. Even his divorce lawyer (another Christian) condemned my soul to hell because of my hardhearted refusal to try still another reconciliation.

"Even now, seven years later, no one believes the story. And at this moment he has my daughter, thanks to a court order and gross misunderstanding of a letter she wrote to [a nationally known Christian counselor]. . . . My daughter, now eleven, is reduced to the almost suicidal state I was in. She desperately wants out."

"I did not leave until after his third murder attempt on me and still I believed in a reconciliation. I kept thinking that if I would do right things, he wouldn't get angry. He never even admitted abuse. Our marriage was so 'perfect' on the outside that few people believed that I had been abused."

"It's been four months since my husband was removed from our home by police, and most people who know about it just pass judgment on me. You don't know what it's like to wake up at three A.M. with your husband standing over you, not talking, not doing anything, just staring at you. You don't know how guilty you feel or just plain confused when people you love don't help or won't get involved. You can't know my fears as a mother of three boys, of beginning to lose the respect of my sons. I can still hear my husband screaming at me, 'You're a Christian and God wants us together. You leave me and nothing will go right in your life forever.' "

Those are the words of Christian women. Women who married with dreams about what it would mean "to have and to hold . . . till death us do part." Women to whom the thought of facing death at the hands of their husbands was incomprehensible—until the violence began.

Then they were choked, spat on, pulled by their hair across the floor. They suffered broken ribs and arms, perforated eardrums, concussions, kidney damage and internal hemorrhaging. They are joined by thousands of other Christian women who are still being victimized by their husbands and by untold others who, though not physically abused, have known unrelenting mental abuse.

In a "Focus on the Family" radio program that has been broadcast several times, James Dobson paints a very different picture of "one of the most common causes of wife abuse" than what has emerged from our research and talks with battered women.

Here's the situation. The husband is not a very verbal person and is rather passive. He's not meeting his wife's needs. She is deeply angry about this and her approach is to bludgeon the tar out of him. She's not pulling him toward her, she is hammering him verbally. He can't handle that verbally. He cannot hold his own with her in words because she's a far more verbal person than he. . . . And she is tearing him and she is attacking him and she is just giving him what with all the time. And finally he gets so frustrated that the only thing he knows to do is to respond with power and he turns around and beats her up.[3]

It is alarming that the man who is undoubtedly the most widely esteemed Christian psychologist in the country today would publicly state that most batterers don't want to beat up their wives and respond with "the only thing he knows to do . . . and beats her up." To present such a picture of a typical abusive marriage is misleading. Men who batter their wives are often articulate, function successfully in their jobs and are competent in their roles outside of marriage. They come from all walks of life—businessmen and pastors, architects and authors, farmers and carpenters—and many hold positions of leadership. In fact, one recent study found that more highly educated batterers inflicted more serious injuries.[4]

Furthermore, violence is not legislated by the wife's actions; it is a specific choice made by the abusive husband. The primary focus of therapy with abusive men is to help them recognize that they do not have only one response option. If frustrating situations offered only one option, abusers would be equally violent on the job, driving in traffic, or interacting with friends; but that is simply not true. The majority of abusers direct their violence specifically and purposely toward their wives.

None of this is to imply that Dobson is uncaring toward victims of wife abuse. In his book *Love Must Be Tough,* he advocates the principle of "loving toughness" in dealing with a variety of marital problems, including wife abuse. Making a distinction between "being a confident, spiritually submissive woman and being a *doormat,*" he says that to teach that God won't allow anything wrong to happen to you as long as you're submissive is "Pollyanna in the pulpit."[5]

In considering the situation of Laura, a battered wife, Dobson recommends that she "break out of that tyranny while she's still young enough to cope with the consequences. This might be accomplished by forcing the matter to a crisis. . . . Counselors suggesting that this frightened woman remain passive and submissive despite the abuse should have to look into Laura's eyes and tell her that in person. I don't believe anyone should be required to live in that kind of terror, and in fact, to do so is to tolerate a behavior which could eventually prove fatal to the marriage, anyway."[6]

The fact that Dobson periodically addresses the issue of wife abuse in his speaking and writing is commendable in itself. But he does appear to vacillate between a concern for the woman and a need to hold the victim at least partially responsible for her victimization. In *Love Must Be Tough* he writes, "I have seen marital relationships where the woman deliberately 'baited' her husband until he hit her. This is not true in *most* cases of domestic violence, but it does occur."[7] Though he says this is true less than half the time, he devotes as much space to women who "bait" as he does to those who are "victims in the true sense of the word."[8] He comments:

> Why, one may ask, would *any* woman want to be hit? Because females are just as capable of hatred and anger as males, and a woman can devastate a man by enticing him to strike her. It is a potent weapon. Once he has lost control and lashed out at his tormentor, she then sports undeniable evidence of his cruelty. She can show her wounds to her friends who gasp at the viciousness of that man. . . . In short, by taking a beating, she instantly achieves a moral advantage in the eyes of neighbors, friends, and the law. . . . I have seen women belittle and berate their husbands until they set them aflame with rage. . . . Finally, the men reach a point of such frustration that they explode, doing precisely what their wives were begging them to do in the first place. . . . Victims in the true sense of the word . . . may think I am suggesting that they are responsible for their husband's violence. Not so! But domestic violence has more than one source of motivation, and that fact should be admitted.[9]

Nowhere, unfortunately, does Dobson consider how baiting fits into the cycle of violence itself. By "baiting" their husbands, battered wives move through a frightening period of escalating emotional tension and into the time of calm and contrition that often follows a violent outburst.

In a 1988 radio interview with former abuser Paul Hegstrom and his wife, Judy, Dobson stated that believing in the concept of submissiveness "does not mean that a man has a right to beat up his wife." And apparently indicating the need for a theology that gives greater emphasis to the responsibility of husbands, he asked, "To what degree does our theology sometimes seem to support abusiveness of the wife?"[10]

While interviewing the Hegstroms, Dobson turned the emphasis to Judy with questions like, "What did it take to make Paul blow up? What did you have to do? Did you have to push him pretty hard or could you not avoid it?" The interview repeatedly focused on Judy's responsibility in the matter with statements such as "Were you what we call an enabler—someone who really makes it possible for an abusive person to do their thing?" And "Really, Judy was cooperating with you, Paul, in this abusive problem. . . . What you needed for her to do was to draw a line for you. That kind of . . . doormat personality that says 'Walk on me, just don't leave me,' actually antagonizes the problem. It doesn't solve it. It makes it worse."[11]

Here, as with many pastors to whom battered Christian women have turned for counsel, Dobson appears dangerously close to blaming the victim for her own victimization. From our work with battered women, we would contend that if the church errs on any side, it should be on the side of the powerless, the victim. For too long it has focused on the woman's responsibility for her husband's behavior rather than on calling the abuser to accountability and change.

When one analyzes the problem of wife abuse by blaming the victim, the formula for action, says psychologist William Ryan, becomes extraordinarily simple: Change the victim.[12] According to this logic, if we could just get that nagging wife to stop carping at her husband, she'd no longer be dragged across the floor by her hair. Or if the tardy wife would just serve dinner on time, her husband would cease bloodying her nose.

A problem arises, however, when one considers what the data says: most battered women don't know what triggers their husbands' violence. That's part of the terror. The women have no idea when the abuse will occur, what will precipitate it. If they did, they would be the first to change. There's no masochistic joy in getting choked, stabbed, burned and bruised. Unfortunately, many women become almost obsessive in their attempts to figure out what they're "doing wrong," despite their powerlessness in controlling their husband's outbursts.

When counselors, pastors and the church blame the victim, they unwittingly become part of the problem. In shifting the focus from abuser to victim, the victim is held responsible for the abuser's violence at a time when she most needs to be empowered. This, in turn, further debilitates a woman whose self-confidence and self-esteem are already depleted. Constantly scanning her environment for clues and mistrusting her own actions, she is caught in an endless thought process of wondering just what she did to cause the violence.

Caricatures, such as the one that most battered women have verbally bludgeoned and hammered their husbands into action, can provide a convenient means for the Christian community to wash its hands of any responsibility in the matter of wife battering. These stereotypes become an embedded perspective trickling down from Christian leader to local pastor to ordinary churchgoer.

What this ultimately means, as Russell and Rebecca Dobash point out, is that the problem of wife abuse can be ignored without any feeling of guilt. "If the woman is 'used to the violence,' 'doesn't mind it,' or even 'seeks it,' then why should people go out of their way to help her or lose any sleep over the fact that they have done nothing or have failed to respond to her request for help?"[13]

A Challenge to Masochism

The belief that any woman—victim or otherwise—in some unconscious way brings on her own abuse was a particularly influential view within psychiatry and social work during the 1940s and '50s. This perception of women as innately masochistic emanated from the work of Sigmund Freud, who proposed that, for women, masochism was "the preferred state."[14] Masochism, "the condition in which sexual gratification depends on suffering, physical pain and humiliation,"[15] was basic to Freud's feminine psychology; it became for him an essentially feminine behavior and an expression of the feminine nature. As a result of Freud's influence, masochism, passivity and femininity became closely associated and were for many years widely accepted as accurate descriptions of basic female character. This view predisposed many professionals to perceive violence toward women as inevitable and to believe that women who experienced such violence unconsciously provoked or enjoyed it.

In recent years, however, Freud's theory of masochism has been seriously examined and widely rejected as an explanation for why women are victimized. While we would grant that there are *both* women and men who might be identified as masochists, no causal link has been established between masochism and wife abuse. Since empirical documentation of true masochism is rare (and alternate explanations are almost always more sensible), we would argue that more sophisticated and complete analysis of most seemingly masochistic situations would yield a much different explanation than that the person was deriving sexual gratification from pain and humiliation. As an explanation for why a woman would tolerate abuse, masochism simply fails to address the full range of social, religious and psychological variables.[16] It is a myth that is clinically naive and will not stand up in the face of empirical evidence.

In their study of battered women, traditionally thought by clinicians to have enjoyed or brought on their beatings, researchers Don Dutton and Susan Lee Painter discovered that women stayed with their abusers for reasons very different from those offered by Freudian psychology:

> The beatings leave the women exhausted, emotionally and physically hurt and drained, and thus in more than usual need of some human warmth and comfort. In this particularly needy state, the men who have just abused them are often still there and sometimes even feeling guilty. Thus, whatever warmth or affection these men offer tends to be accepted by the women, simply because they are in need. . . . It is not the abusive side of their abusers to which these women bond but rather to the warmer, affectionate side that meets their needs to be loved and cared for.[17]   .

It is a myth that battered women deserve to be beaten or that they cause the violence by provoking their men beyond a tolerable point, says psychologist Lenore Walker. Often people recall situations in which the woman "seemed to deserve what she got: she was too bossy, too insulting, too sloppy, too uppity, too angry, too obnoxious, too provocative, or too something else."[18] The assumption is that if the woman had changed her behavior, the batterer would have stopped his violence. But Walker found that most women "stated that they were taken unaware by the violence demonstrated by their men" and could not have predicted that the men would have been so violent.

Walker suggests instead "that a combination of sociological and psychological variables account for the existence of the battered-woman syndrome."[19] Battered women, she says, do not select abusive situations because of some personality deficit, but develop certain distortions as a result of the battering. Applying her theory of "learned helplessness" to the behavior of battered women, Walker posits that the process of victimization entraps an abused wife by creating a "psychological paralysis" which inhibits her from leaving the relationship.

Repeated batterings, like electrical shocks, diminish the woman's motivation to respond. She becomes passive. Secondly, her cognitive ability to perceive success is changed. She does not believe her response will result in a favorable outcome, whether or not it might. Next, having generalized her helplessness, the battered woman does not believe anything she does will alter any outcome. . . . Finally, her sense of emotional well-being becomes precarious.[20]

The coercive control of the abusive husband has been noted by those who work with victims and compared to the "brainwashing" situations of hostage victims or those in religious cults. The long-term effect of the repeated and unpredictable situations of terror to which battered women are subjected is that they become afraid of staying in their marriages and yet are terrified of leaving.

The Myth Lives On
While the validity of Freud's theories has been challenged both by

empirical research and philosophical critique, the myth of masochism and the nature of women lives on. A *Time* cover feature on domestic violence in 1983 mentioned the belief, still held by many men and even many women, "that abused wives have a masochistic streak that keeps them in the home long after the beatings have begun."[21]

Unfortunately, this is also a view underlying much of the advice given women within Christian circles. One clear example can be found in the writings of Paul Meier and Frank Minirth, a team of psychiatrists associated with Dallas Theological Seminary. In their book *Happiness Is a Choice,* they state in an edition that has gone through over two dozen printings and is available in tens of thousands of copies:

> Whenever a battered wife comes seeking advice and consolation because her husband beats her up twice a week, our usual response is, "Oh, really! How do you get him to do that?" In all the scores of cases of this nature that we have analyzed in depth, there was only one case in which the battered wife was not provoking (usually unconsciously) her explosive husband until he reached the boiling point (of course, this does not diminish the husband's responsibility). After a beating, the husband feels very guilty and spoils his wife for several weeks. In the meantime, she is getting from people around her the sympathy which she craves, *and she is satisfying her unconscious needs to be a masochist.*[22] (Italics added)

To identify women who experience violence from their husbands as masochistic not only defuses much of the moral outrage that should be felt in response to the abuse itself, but it also severely minimizes the husband's responsibility for his actions. Clinging to masochism as a viable explanation for wife abuse dismisses the fact that for the most part battered women are guilty of doing exactly the opposite of what Meier and Minirth indicate: they generally do not seek sympathy but keep their abuse private—thus wife battering's common label, the "silent crime." Despite the parenthetical acknowledgment by these men that the abuser bears some responsibility for what he has done, they actually hold the woman accountable for her own abuse.

Apparently recognizing the need to soften their position, Meier and Minirth have recently revised this paragraph in *Happiness Is a Choice* so that in its thirty-third printing it now reads:

In some cases when a battered wife comes seeking advice and consolation because her husband beats her up twice a week, we have to wonder if there is a possibility that she has a passive-aggressive personality and is subconsciously provoking his explosive behavior.

Even in revised form, however, their position remains substantially unchanged and clinically incorrect. What is perhaps most telling is the fact that in a one-paragraph summary of the complex issue of wife abuse, they focus only on the woman who is "satisfying her unconscious needs to be a masochist."

Looking for a Way Out

Closely related to the masochism myth is the idea that many battered women find in their abuse the long-sought way out of troubled marriages. On the 1984 "Focus on the Family" program cited earlier, James Dobson championed such a view. He charged:

I've seen situations where the wife, I think, wanted most to be beaten up. There is a certain moral advantage that comes from having been hit by this man. Then you're in charge, you're self-righteous, you can leave, you have your exit. You want out, you can't find a moral way out because the Bible says marriage is forever, and if you can just push that guy until he turns around and blacks your eye, then boy the whole world, God included, can see that you were the one that's right and you were the one that was taken advantage of, and all of a sudden you're the martyr.

Dobson's observation that some battered women want to be beaten up as an excuse for getting out of their marriage is a perspective that runs counter to our findings with battered Christian women. In fact, the full weight of clinical research on domestic violence consistently

confirms the opposite: Women repeatedly return to abusive relationships hoping to resolve the conflict and thus to not see themselves or
their marriages as failures. Terry Davidson warns that the battered
woman is "pathetically eager" to believe her husband's promise of
reform. She will often take advantage of help just to get through a
crisis and then go back to her husband once the tension has sub-
sided.[23]

In interviews with battered women, Rebecca and Russell Dobash
found that many victims were forgiving of their aggressors, particularly
after the initial beating. The women often reacted to the violence they
had received by returning home with high expectations for change.
"Why did I go back?" asked one respondent. "Oh, because he gave me
so many promises that it was unbelievable. . . . Because I was sure
there was something in me that could make the marriage work. I was
quite positive about that. . . . It might have been just a period he was
going through, you know."[24]

From her two-year study of battered women, sociologist Kathleen
Ferraro identified six *techniques of neutralization* used by victims,
ways they minimize or dismiss the violence in order to remain with
or return to violent men. Those techniques include attempting to
"save" the abuser from himself, acknowledging the abuse but attrib-
uting it to external forces, dismissing the violence as "no big deal,"
assuming responsibility for the violence ("I was nagging him"), denying that there are any options for leaving and appealing to higher
loyalties, such as a belief that violence is no grounds for divorce.[25]
Rather than looking for an easy way out of their abusive marriages,
battered women generally work hard at trying to neutralize the violence and stay in their marriages.

Praying for Change
Battered women are more accurately represented by the Florida woman
who remains married, despite years of abuse to herself and her chil-

dren, "because it's biblical. You don't read in Scripture 'if this' or 'if that' you can get out of marriage."

Approximately seventy-five per cent of the nearly 100 battered women in our sample stayed with their abusive husbands long after most would consider it wise. Rather than leave, they prayed for change in their husbands or for the ability to endure the abuse. Those who left generally did so after years of questioning whether or not there was adequate biblical justification for divorcing an abusive spouse.

One of those women has been abused extensively during her twelve years of marriage. She has had teeth knocked out, suffered a brain concussion and tailbone injury, and been subject to degrading sexual abuse. Yet she continues in the relationship "because I tell myself that maybe it won't happen again. I do remind myself, though, that with the last violent scene, I almost didn't have to fear another time. I literally thought I was through."

For many victims, the price of staying is extremely high. A grief-stricken mother from Kansas wrote, "My daughter stayed with her husband, against my advice, and it cost her her life. There was an argument and it led to an apparent taking of her own life. She suffered terrible verbal as well as physical abuse for almost twenty-four years. It is fatal if allowed to run its course. Breaking up a home is far better than losing a precious loved one."

Disapproval from the Church
Most of the women in our sample found little sympathy or support within the church after revealing their abusive situations to others. "One pastor I counseled with said he was sure I must be doing something to cause the violence," claims a woman still married to her abusive husband. "That's what my mother thought until she was here and he threatened to kill her because of my poor housekeeping."

Said an Arizona woman, physically abused for the duration of her five-year marriage, "I have become angry at many Christians' attitudes toward abuse, the same attitudes I used to have—that I was mainly responsible and that by my love and submission I could change him. It has been a hellish experience and much of the pain has come from the disapproval of other Christians. I wish the church would begin emphasizing personal responsibility more. We are not responsible for each other's sins. We can aggravate a problem, but a woman cannot make her husband hit her! I wish Christians could be encouraged to respect the decisions of abused wives. Only they know all the data."

Susan Brooks Thistlethwaite, a theology professor at the University of Chicago, contends that "women with a violent spouse have believed that the Bible actually says what they have been taught it says—that women are inferior in status before husband and God and deserving of a life of pain." While women may accept this viewpoint through many episodes of violence, she says, eventually *some* women come to an awareness that the violence against them is wrong, oftentimes because the husband begins to abuse the children. "But no sooner do women in violent relationships begin to develop an ideological suspicion that their subordination is wrong," continues Thistlethwaite,

> than they are told that resistance to this injustice is unbiblical and unchristian. They are told that Christian women are meek and that to claim rights for themselves is the sin of pride. Some women at this point cease to struggle further. Some continue to struggle but abandon the church. . . . Some in fact do come to a new herme- neutic and begin to apply it to the Scriptures with the incredible discovery not only that the Bible does not support battering of wives, but that the Scriptures are more on the side of such women than they had ever dared hope.[26]

Representative of those women who, because of their suffering, have seen Scripture as more on their side "than they ever dared hope" is a woman from New England, the victim of fifteen years of physical and verbal abuse at the hands of her minister-husband.

I believe that all things work together for good to those who belong to Christ. Because of that belief, I sought long and hard to work out the problems of verbal and physical abuse before seeking a divorce. I thought that God would surely answer prayers to solve the problems without divorce. . . .

It was hard to cope with "failure" of the marriage because I thought most of the responsibility rested on my shoulders. My ex-husband, confessing to be a Christian and a trained minister, used to say that women "liked to be hurt" and that I was either strange or telling lies when I would tell him that I did not like such treatment. He used to hide behind the fact that I made him angry and I was responsible for his physical violence.

Christian women have been told too long that keeping the marriage together is their responsibility. It has not always been told in outright words, but it has been there. Christian homes would not be in such a mess if the man had been more caring, more "do unto others," more loving and less demanding.

It has been a long road because the church did not seem to have answers for one of its ministers and his family. The church, as usual, is lagging behind the situation rather than being the leader. And some of us have suffered greatly.

How desperately we need to see that mutual submission in marriage and
the family is not subtraction of wifely submission, but the addition
of husbandly submission. Only that is the perfect biblical equation. In
decision making within marriage, the "one" who makes
the decisions should be the "two become one."

Gretchen Gaebelein Hull[1]

Hierarchical marriage . . . constantly teeters on the edge of God's boundary.
. . . It operates too close to where temptation is difficult to resist.

Peter W. Keely[2]

6
Wife Abuse and the Submission of Women

When Ginny first became a Christian, she heard about sub-mission—for women—everywhere she went. In vain Ginny tried applying what she heard to her relationship to her raving and violent husband. "The biggest reason I stayed in the marriage was faith that God could change my husband because God had changed me so much," she acknowledged.

Ginny believed that God would transform her marriage if she was submissive enough. "I guess I was doing the best I could with the knowledge I had. Then I called it faith. Now I would call it delusion, denial or codependency." The verbal and physical abuse worsened and soon became directed toward Ginny's children. Finally she separated from her husband, eventually divorcing him.

"Satan is the big deceiver, the father of all lies, and we Christians have again swallowed a big lie that wives must submit to anything," Ginny said in retrospect. "So many of us—pastors included—have been raised in sick, judgmental, blaming, legalistic homes. I know that a woman is blessed if she submits to a *loving* husband. But if we heard as much teaching on the husband's responsibility to love as we've heard on women submitting, women wouldn't keep getting 'whipped' by that verse on submission."

The connection which many battered women make between their ability to suffer violence from their husbands and their Christian commitment reflects, we believe, what is widely taught within evangelical churches about the submission of women in marriage. It is a perspective which makes women more susceptible to violence and heightens the likelihood that battered women will remain in abusive relationships long after they should.

The Submissive Wife
Christian wives often hear that they were created to serve their husbands. And when the word *submission* is mentioned, it is usually a given that what is being said relates exclusively to women. Being "in submission" has become the standard of what it means to be a godly woman.

Rarely are the men who preach this message deliberately trying to "put down" women. Most are parroting a deeply entrenched view which they have not critically or creatively examined. But what is required from a biblical standpoint for a wife to be considered submissive? And how should she function in marriage? What, if any, are the risks of asserting that marriage cannot be peaceful, much less fulfilling, unless the wife understands her proper role and the husband functions as final decision-maker in all areas?

At one extreme are those who contend that Scripture teaches that the husband "functions as God" and the wife is to obey him "as if he were God himself."[3] At the other end of the continuum are those who either want to "put the notion of submission behind us as a first century hermeneutic"[4] or want to reject Scripture completely because of the centrality of submission, as modeled by Christ, to Christian theology.

A battered woman's understanding of the principle of submission will have a profound impact on how she responds to abuse. To a woman who has tried submitting to a physically and emotionally abusive husband for years and then sees her marriage end in divorce, any talk about "submissive wives" can bring on waves of guilt. After all, how much abuse must one endure to qualify as a truly submissive wife? And how do Christians resolve the tension that arises from the fact that submission is a biblical mandate and yet research reveals that submission by battered women may actually provoke abuse?

Two examples from opposite ends of the spectrum reveal the struggle that Christian women face as they try to submit to their husbands. One woman, divorced, looks back with regret on her ten years of marriage to an abusive man, "especially because of the lasting effect they had on my daughter. . . . I learned from my mother to be submissive and cater to every whim of a demanding, childlike man. I thought I needed him to take care of me, and I also felt sorry for him and thought I could help him through my love and understanding. I see now that he is a rigid, depressed, impulsive man who acts in vengeful, hurtful ways to those closest to him."

The other, married to a non-Christian man who hasn't spoken to her for a year "except for filthy language," is convinced that God wants her to stay in her marriage—no matter what. "I know he has so much bitterness and anger in him that he could kill me, but my greatest hope is that he will be saved. I'm his only source of being saved. If he kills me it doesn't really matter." Although her parents and Christian friends have urged her to leave, the woman "doesn't want any guilt" from being the one to initiate a divorce. "I believe God wants me there," she said, "and I'm scared to do anything that is wrong."

Submit Despite the Violence

Over two-thirds of the women with whom we've talked said they felt it was their Christian responsibility to endure their husband's violence. In so doing they would be expressing a commitment both to God and their husbands. Fifty-five per cent noted that their husbands had said the violence would stop if they would be more submissive; one-third of the women believed that their submissiveness could be the key to stopping the violence.

Over one-third of the women in our sample said they felt pressure from their churches to submit to their husbands despite the violence. One woman noted that she was told by her pastor that her failure to be submissive to her husband was her "only real problem." And an abuse victim from the Midwest, who said that both she and her husband have been Christians for thirty years, wrote to her pastor "asking him to pray that I could endure and that God would bring something from all of this. I've been so depressed. I cry out to God to help me."

It is a popular conviction that by submitting to violence a woman will win her husband to the Lord or, in the case of a Christian husband, help him see the error of his ways. However, accumulating clinical evidence suggests that the single worst action a victim can take is to submit to an abusive partner.

Researcher Megan Jobling asserts that the submissive behavior of battered wives might itself provoke their husbands.[5] And in his book *Family Violence,* George Thorman contends that a battered woman's use of compliance as a coping strategy can be dangerous since in many cases the more submissive she becomes, the more her husband abuses her.[6]

Likewise, Lenore Walker determined from her study of 120 battered women that the religious beliefs of the women "did not protect them from their assaultive men." For many the suffering continued (or even increased) after they were advised by their pastors to submit further. Many of those women later abandoned their religious beliefs.[7]

A 1986 Bureau of Justice Statistics survey concluded that women who report their abusive husbands to the police, rather than those who submitted to the violence, were less likely to be attacked again within the next six months. The survey found that "forty-one per cent of married women who were attacked by their husbands or ex-husbands but did not call the police were assaulted again within an average of six months, compared with fifteen per cent of the women who alerted police."[8]

While the majority of the women in our study felt obligated as Christians to endure violence from their husbands, several regretted— especially for the sake of their children—that they tolerated abuse for so long. A woman, who was subjected to years of physical battering until her marriage ended in divorce, recalled, "I saw the abuse as my part in the suffering of Christ at communion. I wanted to be a redeeming source of love in my husband's life, like Christ. I believed that there was something I should be doing differently." Said another, "I knew I was supposed to be submissive, but I didn't know where to draw the line. I knew everyone had a cross to bear and I thought this was mine."

Absolute Submission
The assumption that the Christian woman's primary responsibility is one of absolute submission to her husband, regardless of what he does or how he acts, is such an automatically accepted tenet of faith for many Christians that it is above questioning. "The primary responsibility for a good relationship in marriage," asserted Reverend Marvin De Hann in the *Good News Broadcaster,* "lies with the wife. If the wife is submissive to her husband, they'll have a good relationship."[9]

Lip service may be given to the biblical call for mutual submission in marriage, but most evangelicals writing on the subject of marital roles would concur with John MacArthur, pastor of Grace Community

Church in Sun Valley, California. "In order for the family to function in harmony, the woman, with no loss of dignity, takes the place of submission to the headship of her husband."[10]

Interpreting what it means for the woman to "take the place of submission," MacArthur says that the husband alone should work outside the home. Basing his interpretation on Titus 2:5 and Ephesians 5, MacArthur states, "I think God is saying that the standard procedure for a wife and a mother is to work inside and not outside the home, and I think it is all related to the principle of being obedient to your own husband."[11]

Submission should be the "welcome response" of Christian women to their husbands, he charges. If a husband "doesn't obey the Word," MacArthur counsels the wife to "submit—submit anyway." Why? Because without her saying anything, "he may be won." And to the woman who is afraid to submit to her husband because he will take advantage of her, MacArthur promises that God will "take care of the results" if there is any abuse. "Wives, as you obey God and submit to your husbands with a gentle and quiet spirit, you can believe God that he will honor your obedience—no matter what."[12]

Basic to MacArthur's view of the woman's role in marriage is his belief that the woman should not have responsibility equivalent to that of the man because by nature she is weaker and is "to be cared for, not left to her own resources."[13] The woman is constantly after man's God-given power, he argues, because she is fallen and fails to realize that "God designed men to be stronger."[14] MacArthur's emphasis on power no doubt emanates from his perception of marriage as "potential warfare." Thus he begins a chapter in his book *The Family* by quoting English World War II Field Marshal Montgomery: "Gentlemen, don't even think about marriage until you have mastered the art of warfare."[15]

Likewise, brothers Paul and Richard Meier assert that "to rank under, to be under obedience," is actually "true freedom for the wife";

any woman who questions such a claim they label "aggressive," "angry" or "rebellious." The husband's role as leader, they explain, includes the making of all final decisions in the home ("there should be nothing that goes on without the husband's awareness or approval") and the establishment of himself as "head over his wife."[16]

In discussing power arrangements in the marital relationship, Paul Meier, Frank Minirth and Frank Wichern of Dallas Theological Seminary quickly dismiss "the symmetrical relationship" by describing it as one in which "differences between two people are minimized. Partners essentially have equal and similar role definitions and tend to mirror each other's behavior sometimes competitively."[17] In contrast, they describe the traditional marriage, most common for Christians, as a "complementary relationship" in which differences are recognized. "The husband devotes himself to his business and has a leadership position in the family. The wife devotes herself to the home and is usually supportive of her husband."[18]

Psychologist Clyde Narramore, long recognized as a pioneer in the field of Christian psychology, asserts that Scripture is crystal clear in calling for submissiveness by wives. Narramore takes the curious position of defending democracy as important while at the same time concluding that domestic democracy will not work. Someone has to assume leadership, he states, and it is the man who should do so; God has set up a "reasonable chain of command" to guide the family.

Narramore acknowledges that this ideal is often unrealized. So he considers the question of what happens when either the husband or the wife is "unable or unwilling" to assume his or her God-given role within the home. Posing the plight of a woman whose husband is "hostile, angry and disturbed"—not the "husband who on rare occasions loses his temper"—Narramore asks, "Is she bound to submit to his angry will?" Narramore's counsel to the victim is to stay; the Bible, he reasons, "does not say, 'Wives, submit yourselves unto your own husbands if they are the kind of men they should be.' " Therefore,

Narramore advises counselors to present the "clear teaching of God's
Word," which is that wives accommodate abusive situations and by so
doing allow themselves to suffer for Jesus and "follow in his steps."[19]

Perhaps the most widely known champion of the "chain of command" perspective on family order is popular conference speaker Bill
Gothard. He too sees abuse as providing a woman with a special opportunity to suffer for Jesus. When asked, "What if a wife is a victim
of her husband's hostility?" Gothard replies, "There is no 'victim' if we
understand that we are called to suffer for righteousness. 'For even
hereunto were ye called: because Christ also suffered for us, leaving
us an example, that ye should follow his steps' (1 Peter 2:21). Christ
was not a victim! He gave his life for us. 'By whose stripes ye were
healed' (1 Peter 2:24). 'Likewise, ye wives . . .' (1 Peter 3:1)."[20]

For Gothard, a wife's submission will be transformed into a God-
honoring, spiritually rewarding experience regardless of the circumstances. "Can a wife claim to be following Scripture," he asks rhetor-
ically, "when she rejects the ministry and rewards of suffering for
righteousness' sake which God calls every Christian to accept (1 Peter
2:18—3:10)?" Urging Christian leaders to stand firm against divorce
and remarriage, Gothard asserts that marital problems will never be
solved "until we have related 'suffering for righteousness' sake' to the
marriage relationship."[21]

Fittingly, Gothard's examples deal only with suffering on the part
of women—not men. In fact, despite the call to mutual submission in
Ephesians 5:21, Gothard says "the philosophy of 'mutual submission'
is a very subtle way of eliminating power. You do this by equally
distributing power to every person; thus no one has any more authority
than anyone else. This is the basis of humanism in which each person
is his own god."[22] For Gothard, "suffering for righteousness' sake" is
not a mutual call to husbands and wives. The rights of women are
rejected in order that the airtight system of male domination not be
disturbed.

There is little evidence that men like Gothard who take Scripture so literalistically are consistent in holding husbands accountable for loving their wives to the degree that they hold wives accountable for submitting. For instance, one of the criteria for aspiring to church office is that the man be "not violent" (1 Tim 3:3), and yet several women in our study noted that while they were repeatedly reminded of their place of submission, the violence of their husbands—deacons, board members and pastors—was overlooked. One minister's wife said that when she revealed the fact of her abuse, "I was even given one strange answer to the passage in Timothy: if we disciplined all the pastors with family problems, there wouldn't be enough pastors to keep the churches open!"

Functionally Unequal

At the heart of such views on submission is the belief that the husband-wife relationship is one of "equality in being, but inequality in function."[23] Women are said to have been created as equal to men yet are functionally to be dependent on men. For example, Meier, Minirth and Wichern assert that if the "husband is the president, the wife should be the vice-president."[24] However, if functionally one is considered an unequal, ontology soon becomes irrelevant. What often happens, either for the sake of so-called stability or to expedite the decision-making process, is that the wife is treated as less than equal.

As Gretchen Gaebelein Hull notes, our analogies about marriage must not be drawn from the world of business and government. Marriage is a relationship, a friendship; the question of who's in charge is irrelevant. "A true friendship is not fraught with deadlocks," she observes. "Just as a friend does not try to 'run the show,' neither will one marriage partner or family member always want to have 'the last word.' Instead, as with true friendship (and in harmony with Philippians 2:4-8), each partner and each family member will want only what is best for the others."[25]

And if deadlocks occur with any frequency in a marriage, a question arises as to how Christian that marriage actually is, she contends. "If the marriage partners are constantly polarized, how can they act as 'one flesh'? Can two walk together, except they be agreed? . . . Any marriage characterized by persistent division and not mutuality of both operation and goals is in trouble. Christian partners are not competitors or adversaries!"[26]

Much of the teaching related to the chain-of-command or hierarchical view is based on assumptions about the meaning of *head* in 1 Corinthians 11:3 ("the head of every man is Christ, and the head of the woman is man, and the head of Christ is God") and Ephesians 5:23 ("the husband is the head of the wife as Christ is the head of the church"). *Head* is taken to mean something on the order of boss, director or master. From that interpretation it is a very short step to espousing the view that man is "head of the *home*," which in turn means he is to be the principal (or sole) breadwinner, make the major decisions for the family, control the finances and discipline the children.

New Testament theologian S. Scott Bartchy charges that too many men have used these "headship" passages as permission to discount other texts calling for mutuality in decision making and the principle of submission. "The models of leadership to which even many Christian males appeal come straight from the battlefields and corporations of the 'Gentile' world," he says.[27]

It is Jesus himself, Bartchy points out, who calls us to examine the ways we use our power and "any satisfaction we may feel with one-sided submission."[28] In Mark 10:22-42 Jesus confronted the presuppositions of male power and dominance: "You know that those who are regarded as rulers of the Gentiles lord it over them, and their high officials exercise authority over them. Not so with you. Instead, whoever wants to become great among you must be your servant, and whoever wants to be first must be slave of all" (Mk 10:42-44).

Similarly, Paul contrasts sharply "the attitudes and actions of a Christian husband to the standard *patria potestas* (absolute power) model of male identity in the first century A.D. A Christian husband is precisely one who has learned so much agape-love from Jesus that he is motivated to control his power to the extent of freely sacrificing himself for the sake of his wife."[29]

The chain-of-command model, on the other hand, reinforces the *patria potestas* view. But, as Richard Foster rightly discerns, "the sting of the teaching [on submission] falls upon the dominant partner."[30] He is to surrender his prerogative to power through self-sacrificing love.

In their research into the meaning of *kephalē* ("head"), biblical scholars Berkeley and Alvera Mickelsen discovered that in ancient Greek it usually did not mean "superior to" or "one having authority."[31] They note that "one of the most complete Greek lexicons, . . . based on examination of thousands of Greek writings from the period of Homer (about 1000 B.C.) to about A.D. 600, which, of course includes New Testament times, . . . does not include 'final authority,' 'superior rank,' or anything similar."[32]

Rather, what emerges is an understanding of *kephalē* as "source" or "beginning." When applied, for instance, to the "difficult passage" of 1 Corinthians 11:2-16, "verse 3 does not seem to teach a chain of command. Paul's word order also shows he was not thinking of chain of command. Christ, head of man; man, head of woman; God, head of Christ. Those who make it a chain of command must rearrange Paul's words." In fact, the Mickelsens continue, in verse 11 "Paul seems to go out of his way to show that he was not imputing authority to males when he says, 'For as woman was made from man, so man is now born of woman.' "[33]

Their concluding questions are provocative: "Has our misunderstanding of some of these passages been used to support the concept of male dominance that has ruled most pagan and secular societies since the beginning of recorded history? Has this misunderstanding also robbed us of the richer, more exalted picture of Christ that Paul was trying to give us?"

We would argue that the chain-of-command perspective is neither a biblical nor a psychologically sound pattern for the marriage relationship. In fact, adoption of such a model can easily set the stage for a woman's victimization. An inordinate emphasis on the principle of wifely submission can cloud the fact that wife abuse is an abominable evil representing a profound disregard for the law of love taught by Christ.

To stress wifely submission in a vacuum devoid of husbandly love can result in a disregard for a woman's report of violence and place the woman and her children in great physical danger. Ultimately, it can perpetuate the cycle of violence. When the painful circumstances of battered women are ignored in order to elevate a legalistic standard, it produces people unable to "rejoice with those who rejoice; mourn with those who mourn" (Rom 12:15).

Furthermore, the degree to which a husband's lack of Christlike, sacrificial love is overlooked is the degree to which a fully biblical marriage languishes. To endorse one-dimensional submission is to reject the whole counsel of Scripture. Practically it means that the sanctity of the woman's personhood is ignored and the view of wife as "property" is perpetuated.

Abuse and the Distribution of Power
Family abuse of any sort is, as sociologist David Finkelhor observes, "the abuse of power . . . where a more powerful person takes advantage of a less powerful one," with abuse gravitating "toward the relationships of greatest power differential."[34] As a case in point, sociologist Jean Giles-Sims notes that the most striking fact about the majority of battered women she investigated was that they "felt powerless."[35] From her contextual analysis of marital equality and violence against

wives, sociologist Kersti Yllo found that the rate of wife-beating in couples where the husband dominated was 300 per cent greater than for egalitarian couples. Yllo concluded that "regardless of context, violence against wives is lower among couples where there is a relative equality in decision-making. . . . In general, domination of decision-making by husbands is associated with the highest levels of violence against wives."[36]

This correlation between violence and the unequal distribution of power was also confirmed in a nationwide study of family violence by sociologists Murray Straus, Richard Gelles and Suzanne Steinmetz. Their study revealed that wife-beating is "much more common in homes where power is concentrated in the hands of the husband. The least amount of battering occurs in democratic homes."[37]

Violence is used by many husbands as a means of legitimatizing their authority and establishing their place as a family decision-maker, these researchers suggest. Inequality in the distribution of power within the family then initiates "a chain reaction of power confrontations running throughout the family."[38] If the husband is violent to his wife, "she may decide not to retaliate physically because she would be even more endangered. Rather than hit her husband, she repeats the pattern toward someone weaker than herself—a child. The child in turn lashes out at brothers and sisters, with the cycle often reaching the ultimate conclusion of the youngest child abusing the family dog or cat."[39] They found the safest homes in terms of all forms of domestic violence were those in which a sharing of power was the norm. The higher the proportion of family decisions shared by husband and wife, the less the likelihood of violence.

Inequality and Conflict

"Mutually enhancing interaction is not probable between unequals," charges psychiatrist Jean Baker-Miller in her examination of domination and subordination. "Indeed, conflict is inevitable."[40] But this

conflict, she notes, is generally hidden in a relationship between unequals because the very existence of conflict is denied; conflict simply
doesn't exist—both in the eyes of those who dominate and for those
who have incorporated "the dominant group's conception of themselves as inferior or secondary"—that is, until it's too late.[41] The dominant group—men—is "usually convinced that the way things are is
right and good, not only for them but for the subordinates."[42]

Women, in turn, are encouraged to develop qualities such as submissiveness, passivity, dependency and lack of initiative. "In general,"
says Miller, "this cluster includes qualities more characteristic of children than adults—immaturity, weakness and helplessness. If subordinates adopt these characteristics they are considered well adjusted."[43]
Women are both "diverted from exploring and expressing their needs"
and encouraged to "transform" those needs into the needs of others—
usually men and children.[44] But that transformation is a most precarious one that "hangs by a delicate thread."

The tragedy of an unequal distribution of power, Miller contends,
is that it deprives both the subordinates and the dominants, particularly on a psychological level. Acknowledging that in our culture serving others "is for losers, it is low-level stuff," Miller makes a strong
case for the fact that submissiveness, vulnerability, adaptability and
cooperativeness are psychological characteristics that are essentials for
healthy living. They are not qualities to be shunned. "In the course
of projecting into women's domain some of its most troublesome and
problematic exigencies, male-led society may have also simultaneously, and unwillingly, delegated to women not humanity's 'lowest needs'
but its 'highest necessities'—that is, the intense, emotionally connected cooperation and creativity necessary for human life and growth."[45]

The gap created between men and women by a hierarchical world
view becomes part of our relational heritage to the point that it defines
our very consciousness of ourselves as men and women. Thus we talk
about the "masculine" or the "feminine" in such a way as to believe

that such characteristics are, and should be, exclusive to each sex. Ultimately such thinking becomes a psychological, relational and spiritual wedge between men and women.

Psychological studies such as those mentioned have much relevance for the Christian community which, for the most part, espouses a distribution of power that puts the man in charge and sees the woman as needing his control. For battered women, the assigning of ultimate authority to men opens the door for husbands to wield power that is characterized by coercive force and unreasonable demands. It is power motivated by lust and pride, seeking its own goals and satisfying its own passions. The Bible is clear that power of this sort is evil (2 Thess 2:7-11; Eph 2:2).

When a man strikes his wife he is using power destructively, regardless of his reasons. Yet how little concern is expressed within the church over this illegitimate use of power by men. Instead the focus is repeatedly turned toward establishing wifely submission as the guarantee of a rewarding, peaceful marriage. We have not let the whole counsel of Scripture inform our understanding of submission, nor have we hearkened to the psychological wisdom of our day which could give us practical ways to understand the existence of wife abuse in our own homes.

Like society at large, the church has failed to establish checks which would identify and confront the misuse of power. The challenge we face is to thoughtfully re-examine interpretations of what Scripture says about power and authority in marriage and to embrace a more comprehensive definition of Christian marriage.

For he is himself our peace, who has made the two one and has
destroyed the barrier, the dividing wall of hostility.

Ephesians 2:14

Never underestimate the demands that forgiving puts on an average
person's modest power to love.

Lewis Smedes[1]

7

The Process
of
Reconciliation

The letter was painful and disheartening. It came from a seminary friend who had recently divorced her abusive husband.

"The divorce was final in July," Judy wrote. "We went to court eight times, all but one Dave's choice. I saw it all as another method of harassment and abuse. I kept faith and treaded water to keep my head up and not down. . . . I got sole custody, but he got one weekday and every other weekend visitation, which means he is over here every three or four days. . . . God is on the throne though. I feel a lot more peace and am glad I am divorced."

They were a couple whom we were confident would "make it." We'd gone to seminary together and worshiped together. We'd played with each others' children, shared meals and Communion and struggled to make sense out of the conflict and violence in their marriage.

Like many of their friends, we had tried to faithfully support and challenge Judy and Dave, hopeful that the combination of prayer, their involvement with a Christian psychologist and accountability to a caring Christian community would make a difference in their marriage. But it didn't. At least not in the way we expected. Divorce was still the outcome. It was anguishing to face the fact that, all other options tried, reconciliation still did not occur.

As we consider the issue of reconciliation in a marriage once characterized by physical and emotional abuse, we offer no easy-to-follow formulas or guarantees of success. We are confident of the healing power of God's love for relationships bruised by abuse. Nonetheless, we must also acknowledge that most often reconciliation does not occur. When it does, it is not an event but a painful and slow process.

In the secular arena, *reconciliation* is an alien term. Rarely is it even mentioned in discussions of domestic violence. To speak of reconciliation is considered tantamount to demanding that the woman stay imprisoned in the cycle of violence—believing her husband's pleas for forgiveness, kissing and making up, praying that things will "really be different this time," then being the object of yet another explosive outburst and seeing the cycle repeat itself.

True reconciliation, however, means anything but maintaining the status quo. When reconciliation is applied to broken relationships it is a radical concept. "Reconciliation often raises new and troubling questions about values, motives, spiritual commitments, forgiveness, accountability, relationships," notes Lynn Buzzard, former executive director of the Christian Legal Society and a leader in Christian conciliation efforts. It is a process of personal responsibility, he continues, not a means of vindication. "There is no more central and powerful theme (or claim) than reconciliation. But just because it is central and powerful, and has to do with all of us in all of our relationships, we are well-warned that the process of reconciliation will mirror the proc-

ess by which it was gained—in Christ. Dying to self is never easy—
but it is the purchase price of reconciliation."[2]

That perspective is echoed by Desmond Tutu, Anglican Bishop of
South Africa and a Nobel laureate for his work for peace.

Reconciliation is not cheap, nor is it an easy option. . . . Who said
reconciliation excludes confrontation? Who says reconciliation is
easy? We must know what we are asking for when we say we must
be ministers of reconciliation, because reconciliation cost God the
death of his son. True reconciliation, my brothers and sisters, is
costly. It involves confrontation because the cross was a confrontation with evil. The cross showed the evil of evil.[3]

There would be no reconciliation were it not for Christ's redemptive
act in history. And, fittingly, the cross provides the model for reconciliation on a relational level. The source of reconciliation is God "who
reconciled us to himself through Christ and gave us the ministry of
reconciliation" (2 Cor 5:18). The substance of reconciliation is a hope
grounded in the fact that Christ overcame death and provided the
avenue for us to be reconciled to God and one another.

Paul talks of reconciliation over against enmity, alienation and other conditions of estrangement from God. God's purpose in reconciling
the world to himself was "making peace," putting "to death their
hostility" (Eph 2:15-16). And the peace which Paul speaks of, when
applied interpersonally, is not a mere ointment to soothe bruised relationships. It is a radical transformation of very damaged relationships
so that strife and estrangement are, under the conviction of the Holy
Spirit, replaced with an agape love and the power to actually see and
treat others differently. Through the process of reconciliation death
and violence have lost their sting, and peace is made available even
in the most chaotic circumstances.

Furthermore, reconciliation is intrapersonal. Through the process of
reconciliation the "violence within" is conquered, and we are set free
from the inner torment and battle which so often lead to interpersonal

conflict. Reconciliation allows not only the restoration of our relationship with God and with one another, then, but also a settling of the score with ourselves. It is the emancipation of our hearts and minds, an inner peace which passes all understanding, a peace that is grounded in and made possible through the cross of Calvary.

The Miracle of Reconciliation

It is no small matter to speak of reconciliation between a victim of physical and emotional abuse and her abuser. "Brutality, no matter who commits it, confronts us with one of the most agonizing crises of forgiveness," says ethicist Lewis Smedes. And forgiveness, he notes, is "a miracle that has no equal."[4] While certain steps can and must be taken if reconciliation is to be set in motion, that true reconciliation involves *healing,* and that is the work of the divine.

" 'Conflict dynamics,' while helpful in talking about conflict and in analyzing its elements, is not very helpful in healing," concludes Lynn Buzzard. "There is an element of mystery and miracle in the entire process, an element of *Kairos* beyond our manipulation. . . . Where the spirit is not willing, the management skills of peacemakers offer only an illusion of reconciliation."[5] Reconciliation is *not* primarily a function of technique or strategy but a process orchestrated by the Holy Spirit. It involves something beyond what can be actualized through human effort alone.

The percentage of reconciliations between wife abusers and their victims is pitifully low. One psychologist who directed a crisis center for battered women likened it to the rehabilitation rate of heroin addicts. "There are success stories," she said, "but they are few and far between." Why is it so difficult to find former abusers who are reconciled with their wives? Certainly one reason is because many abusers don't consider their actions wrong, let alone sinful. But, perhaps more importantly, it is also because physical brutality destroys something vital within a relationship. It is an attack on the essence of the woman.

It is a concrete way of saying that she is worthless. The scars created from such a message run so deep that the restoration of that relationship is difficult indeed.

"I've gone through a grieving process," related a woman who is working toward reconciliation with her husband, "because something has been lost. I feel deep pain over the fact that we never had the kind of marriage we could have. Something was destroyed and I've had to give up the dream that we could ever have it back."

Steps toward Reconciliation

While reconciliation cannot begin until the abuser is truly repentant and remorseful, oftentimes it is action on the part of the victim which forces a batterer to come to that critical juncture. Pressing assault charges, leaving and refusing to consider a return until the abuser has completed a counseling program for offenders, or "going public" with the abuse to employers and relatives may in fact be first steps toward reconciliation, steps which the woman will take as a means of offering her husband yet another opportunity to acknowledge the illegality and the immorality of what he has done. These are acts of both self-preservation and love for her husband. Since he is participating in evil, forcing him to deal with it and not submitting to it is an act of love.

Once she has taken the first step, the victim holds virtually no power over whether or not the batterer will choose the path of reconciliation. That is a matter of the heart—a new heart, given to the one who willingly submits to God's chastisement. And for one who would not submit to his wife "out of reverence for Christ" (Eph 5:21), one who instead chooses to physically and emotionally abuse the person he was commanded to love "as Christ loved the church" (Eph 5:25), such an act of contrition may be far off indeed.

Defilement of this magnitude calls for more than willpower to bring about authentic change. "Willpower will never succeed in dealing with the deeply ingrained habits of sin," admonishes Richard Foster. "The will has the same deficiency as the law—it can deal only with externals. It is not sufficient to bring about the necessary transformation of the inner spirit."[6]

That change must come from God. It is a manifestation of his grace, his gift to those who will receive it. As Dietrich Bonhoeffer elucidates in *The Cost of Discipleship,* while God's grace is free, it is not cheap. "Costly grace is the only pure grace, which really forgives sins and gives freedom to the sinner. Cheap grace is the preaching of forgiveness without requiring repentance."[7]

Grace which cost God the life of his Son requires obedience. "Only those who obey believe," continues Bonhoeffer.[8] And as Foster explains, the way of discipleship is " 'the way of disciplined grace.' It is 'grace' because it is free; it is 'disciplined' because there is something for us to do."[9]

Cheap Grace

One of the major roadblocks to true repentance, however, is that there is often a temptation within the church to avoid conflict or confrontation. How often victims of abuse have been admonished by the Christian community to quickly smooth things over and to offer forgiveness at no cost! But dispensing cheap grace—offering the abuser a shortcut on his painful journey toward the realization of authentic forgiveness—only impedes true repentance and ultimately undercuts reconciliation.

"Some people hinder the hard work of forgiving by smothering confrontation," challenges Smedes. "We should not confuse the technique of smoothing things over with the high act of forgiving those who transgress against us."[10]

Forgiving the abuser is not forgetting what he has done, Smedes continues.

Forgiveness, cheaply given, *is* dangerous, let us face it. If we forgive, we are likely to forget; and if we forget the horrors of the past we are likely to let them happen again in the future. . . . Forgetting, in fact, may be a dangerous way to escape the inner surgery of the heart that we call forgiving. . . . The pains we dare not remember are the most dangerous pains of all. . . . You do not excuse people by forgiving them; you forgive them at all only because you hold them to account and refuse to excuse them.[11]

When a victim of physical abuse confronts the man who has betrayed her with his brutality, she enters into an agonizing process in which her own feelings of anger, rage, fear and loneliness will surface. She must consider whether or not she is willing to forgive. And in doing so, she will meet head-on her longing for vengeance and an inner uncertainty about whether in forgiving she is abandoning any loyalty to her own self. Is she once again accommodating the appetite of an impulsive, angry and needy child who will later lose control, or is she doing the Christlike thing and offering forgiveness? This is the dilemma she faces.

A woman who has stayed with her emotionally abusive husband, attempting to creatively work for change in that relationship, emphasized the need for Christians to hear and accept women like herself rather than sitting in judgment of them. "After twenty years of pain I was in a rage. And what was I supposed to do with all my anger? Continue to stuff it down? That's the exact time you need to be accepted. But so many so-called Christians look at you like you're nuts. They don't know the pain, and getting some of it out is part of the healing. If Christians could only accept you when you're angry, you could get it out, you could work it through." The church must temper its expectations—about how and when an abused woman should forgive her husband—with a strong dose of empathy for what the woman has experienced and a new awareness of the fact that forgiveness and reconciliation are a journey, a process.

Nonetheless, the woman must forgive her husband—not primarily for his sake, but for her own. "If forgiving is a remedy for the wounds of the past," comments Smedes, "we cannot deny *any* human being the possibility of being forgiven lest we deny the victim the possibility of being healed through forgiving."[12]

Just as Paul urged the Corinthian Christians to offer forgiveness to the sinner as an act of obedience that would stop Satan from gaining the advantage over *them* ("For we are not unaware of his schemes"— 2 Cor 2:11), so too the battered woman foils Satan's plans for *her* by forgiving her husband. In doing so she is holding up the standard of agape love over that of justice. While it may mean abandoning herself to a seemingly irrational and unfair course of action, it will make absolute sense if it is judged by the standards of that "still, small voice" within.

Facing the Sin

The victim of abuse can choose to forgive her batterer, both for his sake and for her own, but the work of reconciliation cannot begin until the batterer repents. And repentance is a process. It starts when the batterer spiritually and psychologically faces the awfulness of his actions. There must come that loathing of oneself for one's sins as Ezekiel exhorts: "Then you will remember your evil ways and wicked deeds, and you will loathe yourselves for your sins and detestable practices" (Ezek 36:31). The horrors of the past must be named, not left vague and undefined. Here sin and sickness move from the abstract to the concrete. And, most importantly, the batterer takes responsibility for what he has done.

An ex-convict with deep roots of violence likened his victory over the sins of his past to the healing of the Israelites who were bitten by poisonous snakes when they looked at the bronze image of a snake. "Only as we look at the snakes—the problems we've run from in the past—can God bring healing in our lives," he stated.[13] Confronting one's sins is a vital part of facing the past and gaining mastery over it.

Feeling the Pain

Once the abuser has perceived that his wife's feelings about what he did are true, he begins to feel the pain he has inflicted on others. "The family name of this pain is 'guilt.' "[14] And guilt is something the batterer *should* feel. It is the sign of a repentant spirit.

In his book *Whatever Became of Sin?* psychiatrist Karl Menninger upholds the notion of sin and guilt as appropriate because they "serve as some restraint on aggression." To acknowledge the reality of sin means that one takes personal responsibility for one's actions and hence experiences guilt.

> As an operative term *sin* has this value: it identifies something to be eliminated or avoided. . . . The word "sin" does carry an implication of cost, of penalty, of answerability. The wages of *some* sins are death, without doubt; and the wages of lesser sins, while less than death, are substantial, including reparation, restitution, and atonement. Sinning is never with impunity.[15]

The abuser needs to move from his head to his heart regarding his sin. He must identify with the victim such that his brutality hits him full force. Only then can he move to the next level of repentance.

Confessing the Sin

If the batterer *realizes* what he has done and *feels* what he has done, then he is ready to *confess* what he has done. "Confession," Smedes notes, "is the rumbling of a crumbling heart." The edifice of pride and power begins to crumble. The heart of stone is shattered, and a heart of flesh, one which is transparent and willing to take the risks of intimacy, is born in its place (Ezek 36:26).

For the batterer, confession needs to be made privately, before wife and family, and corporately, before the church body (or its leadership). The latter will be confession that is not easily given. It will serve as an important benchmark of accountability when the temptation toward violence again rears its head.

Promising to Change

Once the batterer sincerely faces his sins, experiences guilt for what he has done and confesses his sin, he is ready for what Smedes calls the final step of repentance: *promise.* "If you know and genuinely feel the wrongness of what you did, you also feel a passionate desire not to hurt again. So you make a promise. . . . You can give no guarantee; the best of us go back on promises. But anyone who has been hurt should expect a sincere *intention,* at least."[16]

Here the batterer must tread very carefully for, as any victim of abuse knows, he has proven himself a master of false promises. In the cycle of violence that has characterized their lives, the husband's violence is generally followed by a period of remorse and contrition, with promises—soon to be broken—that such an outburst will never happen again. Consequently, only a promise which comes after the batterer has faced his sin, felt his wife's pain and then confessed his sin, is a promise to be trusted.

The authenticity of that promise will be tested through the fire of time and circumstances. The victim is right in waiting to see what fruit that promise will bear before reuniting with her husband, regardless of his impatience. A premature reuniting, based on even the most hopeful promises of change, will only put unusual pressure on a fragile relationship.

Relearning

The batterer now faces the awesome obstacle of relearning. Because old habits and patterns of response are eroded gradually, only those who make a commitment to this process in the context of community have much hope of succeeding. The batterer's ability to hold true to his promise of change will be directly proportionate to the degree to which he is connected to a support group of fellow batterers or concerned Christians who will hold him accountable and dare to lovingly confront him. He needs an environment of trust in which he can talk candidly about his progress and failures. He needs to see the power of prayer and transparency modeled for him so that he will eventually risk intimacy and responsibility in his marriage.

Called to Stay

Because violence is destructive and is generated from Satan, it is always right for the Christian to take specific action against it. The violence which a battered woman experiences is never anything other than evil. Nonetheless, her husband's abusiveness does not provide the woman with an automatic release from the marriage commitment. While passive acceptance of evil is never God's will, in some situations God may call a battered woman to stay in her marriage. That does not mean that she should submit to violence or even that she must live with her husband. But it may mean being patient and hopeful through the long process of healing.

It is with considerable reluctance that we even address this subject lest it be misconstrued by some as a blanket endorsement of abused wives staying with their abusers no matter what the cost. The church has already erred on this side in the counsel it has given battered women. To be called to stay in the marriage does not necessarily, and perhaps most often will not, mean living with the abuser. Nor does it mean ignoring his violence. It is an active call, not a passive one. God will not redeem a relationship merely because the wife functions as a punching bag. But redemption can come through the wife's sacrificial love. It may woo the abuser to a point of acknowledging his sin and changing his behavior.

When the woman is called to stay in her marriage, she should not be expected to stand alone. Staying will involve great risks, of which both the victim and the church should be aware. It is our contention that such a call should be submitted to psychologically and spiritually informed counsel within the body of believers. During those dark hours of confusion and groping for equilibrium which come when a woman is contemplating which course of action to take (often with the added pressure of financial need and concern for her children's welfare), it is the church's challenge and privilege to sustain and comfort her, to offer guidance and hope. Unless the church is willing to enter into that situation of suffering with the woman—caring for her physical, emotional and spiritual needs and those of her children—it should not advise her to stay in a relationship where she is subject to degrading and inhuman treatment.

The dilemma facing the woman and her church is not one of deciding whether it is right for her to suffer, but rather, whether God is asking her to stay in the relationship. Will her staying be the avenue through which God will introduce his redemptive power and evil be obliterated? Or is her staying a manifestation of her fear to act or a belief that all she deserves is a life of pain?

Being identified with Christ does result in suffering. But just as there are biblical precedents for enduring suffering, so there are examples of those who left situations of violence because of God's call. "By faith [Moses] left Egypt," the writer of Hebrews notes, "not fearing the king's anger" (Heb 11:27). And Mary and Joseph avoided the wrath of Herod by fleeing, under divine direction, to Egypt (Mt 2:13). Whether in leaving or staying, the battered woman must be motivated by faith, not fear.

The Sins of the Fathers
Violence often permeates a family's lineage like a disease. An imprinting of violence can flow from generation to generation, "punishing the children for the sin of the fathers to the third and fourth generation" (Ex 20:5). Research consistently proves that men who have abusive fathers are much more likely to be abusive toward their wives than are other men.[17] Many abusers seem to have inherited, in both a psychological and a spiritual sense, an ontological predisposition toward violence.

But the abuser, like any sinner, can be adopted through faith in Jesus Christ into a new inheritance that is not dictated by earthly destiny. No longer does the abuser need to be dominated by his inheritance of fear and lust for power. Jesus Christ has exploded the bonds of violence.

Nonetheless, destructive attitudes, fears and patterns of conduct hold captive many men who claim the name of Christ. As antithetical as it is to all that life in Christ implies, there are *Christian* men who beat their wives. Some feel justified in doing so. Others recognize the sinfulness of their actions but feel powerless to stop. For the former, the church needs to engage in an aggressive program of re-education which attempts to right the wrong of years of emphasis on hierarchy and patriarchy. Abusers who feel biblically justified in keeping their wives "in line" through physical and emotional manipulation are exemplary graduates of that pervasive theological school which presents women as unequal to men in standing and function.

For the latter group of batterers, those who want to change but feel unable to do so, forces of spiritual bondage are no doubt at work. These must be confronted by the Christian community. If abusive men are the product of violent input from previous generations and from exposure to spiritual and psychological destructiveness over which they have been powerless, a familial bondage may exist which needs to be broken. The task requires severing not only the bonds of their own habitually violent responses but also those of family history.

The batterer who is the product of violent ancestors—parents, grandparents and so on—needs to recognize how formative that early modeling was with regard to how he deals with frustration and fear.

That inherited bondage will not simply evaporate at the point of salvation. What is required is a process of inner healing, coming to know one's emotional, psychological and spiritual roots. Through therapy, prayer and a reliance on the Holy Spirit for discernment, the batterer can unlock the painful secrets of the past and find freedom

from their grip. Just as the prophet Ezekiel predicted the restoration
of Judah from its condition of apostasy, so too God speaks words of
hope to the abuser:

> I will give you a new heart and put a new spirit in you; I will remove
> from you your heart of stone and give you a heart of flesh. And I
> will put my Spirit in you and move you to follow my decrees and
> be careful to keep my laws. . . . I will save you from all your un-
> cleanness. . . . Then you will remember your evil ways and wicked
> deeds, and you will loathe yourselves for your sins and detestable
> practices. (Ezek 36:26-31)

It takes more than will power and reprogramming to change evil habits. Christ breaks the bonds of violence by the work of the Holy Spirit,
purifying what was corrupt. Jesus establishes a new capacity for life
and righteousness. He became the abuser's peace. The batterer's hope
lies not in a formula but in Jesus Christ.

The abuser must actively appropriate the power that is his. "But just
as he who called you is holy, so be holy in all you do," Peter says (1
Pet 1:15). There is work that must be done: honestly facing the evils
of the past so that they can be disarmed, offering that heart of stone
to God for a heavenly heart transplant, entrusting oneself to the care
of those who can help identify destructive habits and offer guidance
for establishing healthy, godly patterns. This and more is the task
which faces the abuser who sincerely desires to be reconciled to his
wife and to the body of Christ.

The biblical message to people embroiled in situations of domestic
violence—the abuser, the abused, the family, the church—is that despite the reign of violence in the past, Christ has broken down every
wall and has become their peace. It is a message of victory and hope.

The suddenness of the provocation does not make me an ill-tempered man; it only shows me what an ill-tempered man I am.

C. S. Lewis

———————————

8

Marriage, Divorce and Wife Abuse

Facing the fact of wife abuse in Christian homes is frightening. It requires that we critically examine a belief rooted in our understanding of Scripture that previously seemed so clear. Marriage is for keeps, we say. But suddenly we find ourselves acknowledging that there are no easy answers to the dilemmas Christians face.

Is a husband's violence in itself a breach in the marriage commitment? Does his violence and refusal to change ever release his wife from the marriage? What about the husband who does invest himself in change and authentically confesses his sin of abuse? Does his confession obligate his wife to be reconciled to him?

These are some of the thorny issues pastors face as they work with abusive families. One stance is to encourage separation but still preach a hard line against divorce, based on the assumption that God sees a substantial difference between the two. But the issue is complicated by the fact that after separation many abused women return to their husbands and face further physical abuse. The marriage is no more God-honoring than before the separation. In exchange, the wife has given up the only real leverage she has for getting her spouse to change. Or, more often, the separation results in the woman realizing that her marriage is dead and that a legal divorce is merely a formal acknowledgment of this fact. Those who do counsel victims to separate must recognize that the separation will lead to scrutinizing the marriage in a new light, a light which may reveal a dead marriage and a desire by the woman to move on. Because divorce occurs more frequently in cases of abuse, pastors and counselors must accept that fact and struggle with the theological and psychological implications in advance.[1]

Living with Injustice

As we examine our opinions and theories about marriage, we engage in a process which philosophers of science would label a "paradigm shift"—a radical restructuring of how we view the world. This time, however, the revolution centers on the time-honored institution of marriage. Elizabeth's painful story provides a clear example of that process at work. What she experienced in her abusive marriage eventually forced her to re-examine Scripture concerning the sanctity of marriage and personhood.

Soft-spoken and shy, Elizabeth married a promising Christian young man after graduating from a Christian college. They settled down, started a successful business and had three beautiful children, a lovely ten-room home and two cars in the garage.

That's the pretty half of the story. The ugly half was all about evil— physical violence, harassment, emotional cruelty. "I didn't talk about it to anyone because I learned growing up that if you can't say something nice about people, you don't say anything at all," Elizabeth recalled. "I couldn't talk about the abuse to anyone without talking about my husband." And when Elizabeth did talk about the problems in her marriage, she wasn't heard. "My father felt I should stay in my marriage come hell or high water. He could not hear me when I said, 'I literally will die if I stay.' He said, 'Oh, Don is just teasing.'

"As a child, I learned a song that I unconsciously used as a structure for my life. Jesus was first, others next and myself last. The song said that if I put myself last I would have J-O-Y. This structure encouraged me to focus on externals for direction in life. What was most important was to please God and others. By the time I had done that I usually didn't get around to figuring out what I wanted or thought.

"I learned that it was better to prefer others to myself and that it was pleasing God for me to serve others. My focus was on being sensitive to others, and I lost perspective of the fact that I was as important as others, that my needs, wants and ideas were equally valuable."

When Elizabeth married, she immersed herself in serving Don and, later, their children. "When I chose who I would marry, I prayed and put out a fleece to be sure that my will and God's matched," she said. "I believed that marriage was a lifetime commitment—till death us do part—and that if God chose a marriage partner for me, it would have to be a good marriage. I was confident that we would live 'happily ever after' and our union would 'count for the kingdom.' When Don became abusive I prayed and believed that God would change him. If God had purposed this marriage, I reasoned, certainly God would take some responsibility and intervene on my behalf. God to the rescue."

Elizabeth was determined to make her marriage work. So she flew across the country to attend a Bill Gothard conference. "The effect was that I became more passive," she said. "I learned verses like 'God will turn the heart of the king.' My responsibility was to love, love, love and to give, give, give. My part was to submit to God and my husband

and let them be the leaders. I released my finances—put my husband's name on my bank account—and gave him more power. Later he took advantage and emptied the bank accounts and took the finances. I took a more passive role, believing that God wanted my husband to lead and direct our family."

Neither Elizabeth nor Don saw the other as an equal. "I did not view myself as equal to Don but lesser than he," she said. "I thought that Scripture told me to esteem others more than myself. My husband liked the biblical phrase 'wives submit' and enjoyed reminding me of it when a difference arose. But the more I submitted, serving my husband and family, the more he seemed to scorn me and abuse me verbally, mentally and emotionally."

A very controlled person, Don eventually stopped his physical battering but then only intensified the emotional abuse. "He would find a place where I was weak and harass me. He liked to see me weak. His was more calculated cruelty than explosive rages. He had this property mindset, this view of having ownership over me. His favorite line was 'I bought you.' "

At one point Elizabeth fled for safety and sanity. Then she returned and for six months lived in an isolated hell within her own home. Don controlled who she could talk to, who she could see; mail stopped coming to the house. The emotional abuse escalated. "I was literally willing to die to save my marriage," she said. "But finally I cried out to God, 'Am I crazy or masochistic? This is just sick.' Then I came to the realization that God had created the institution of marriage to serve people, not the reverse. God saw individuals as most important."

Still Elizabeth struggled with whether divorce was justified in God's sight. So she began studying Greek and Hebrew in order to better understand the biblical teaching on marriage. "I believed the verses I had heard at the Bill Gothard seminars because it was Scripture and Scripture doesn't change. But what eventually happened was that my perception of what they meant changed."

When Elizabeth left her marriage, she also left her three daughters, the youngest only three years of age at the time. Ill-equipped for the ugly custody battle she faced, Elizabeth naively believed that truth would win out in the courtroom. "I thought, 'This is a court of justice. Why is his attorney saying those lies about me?' I was so worn down and should never have signed what I did. I loved motherhood, and giving up custody of my three girls was the most traumatic thing I've done in my whole life."

The past several years have been a difficult period of trying to rebuild a broken life. Every attempt to be with the girls meets with Don's resistance. "There have been many times when I've felt like I am going to crack. I know drugs, alcohol and other relationships aren't options for me. I know I couldn't be clean before God taking those up. When the pain surfaces, the aloneness, sometimes I feel like my body doesn't have any skin on it, like my nerves are all exposed.

"I have come to the realization that life is unjust in many ways. The deck is stacked. But I can't spend my life fighting it. I thought God would vindicate me: God is a just God and my children should be with me. Yes, God would like there to be justice but maybe in this life we have to accept the reality that evil prospers."

The Broken Covenant
The damage of physical and emotional abuse on a marital relationship is often far deeper and more irreparable than can be imagined. Scripture itself informs us that violence causes a profound break in a relationship. "My companion attacks his friends; he violates his covenant," says the psalmist. "His speech is smooth as butter, yet war is in his heart; his words are more soothing than oil, yet they are drawn swords" (Ps 55:20-21). What an apt description of the abuser—smooth speech covering a heart of darkness. And such deceptiveness and violence violate the covenant, we are told.

When you talk about divorce to a Christian woman who is the victim

of physical abuse, more often than not she will cite Malachi 2:16—
" 'I hate divorce,' says the LORD God of Israel"—as a major reason for
why she is staying in her marriage. Many victims have heard sermons
preached against divorce on the basis of that verse or have been counseled to submit to their abuser because "God hates divorce." And
almost without exception, those very women are shocked when they
find out what the last half of that verse proclaims: " 'and I hate a man's
covering himself [or his wife, notes the NIV] with violence as well as
with his garment,' says the LORD Almighty." "Why haven't I heard
anyone preaching about that?" asked one amazed woman.

The violence which an abusive husband perpetrates against his wife
is a betrayal of his oath to love, honor and commit himself to her, a
truth clearly revealed in that same Malachi passage in which God
clarifies just why tearful prayers and offerings will go unheeded: "The
LORD is acting as the witness between you and the wife of your youth,
because you have broken faith with her, though she is your partner,
the wife of your marriage covenant." That break in faith is the outgrowth of a spirit of violence.

A husband's violence toward his wife always offends the covenant
partnership that is under the rule of God's love, and may in some
situations indicate that the couple no longer has what scripturally can
be identified as a marriage. The divine intent for marriage is that it be
an inviolable unity which places man and woman within a permanent
"one flesh" relationship (Gen 2:24). Marriage is based on the divine
command of God (Mt 19:6) and is "the result of a divine determination,
which is understood by those who enter into the relation as a divine
calling, or vocation (cf. Matt. 19:11; I Cor. 7:17)."[2]

The decision to commit oneself to marriage is always a serious act
and one that stands in the shadow of God's action in affirming it
("what God has joined together"—Mt 19:6). Yet the decision to be
violent toward one's spouse is an equally serious act and one which
severely offends the marital union (Mal 2:14-16). Theologian Ray An-

derson poses a vital question at the heart of this issue: "If, in fact, a marriage relationship has utterly failed to live in any semblance of a covenant/partnership such that the integrity of human life is not sustained, but rather is being destroyed, then the question has to be asked: what does God's judgment mean on such a relation?" For the answer, Anderson points to Karl Barth:

> In certain cases, the Word of God may contain a No and powerfully and authoritatively express the final condemnation of a marriage, so that one is forced to conclude that the marriage itself no longer is undergirded (if it ever was) by the divine command. In this case, dissolution by divorce is a recognition of the fact that God has already brought the marriage under the judgment of nonexistence.[3]

Ongoing violence by a husband toward his wife would, in our opinion, be such an offense to the integrity of human life. Ultimately violence destroys both the marriage and the victim. The letter to the Hebrews says that marriage should be "honored by all, and the marriage bed kept pure, for God will judge the adulterer and all the sexually immoral" (Heb 13:4). If we understand fidelity to imply much more than sexual faithfulness and to encompass the honoring of one's partner in a life-giving way, marital violence becomes a manifestation of infidelity. It promotes chaos and death rather than life; it is an example of unfaithfulness to the basic command of love.

Evelyn and James Whitehead, a Catholic psychologist-theologian team, speak to this issue in their book *Marrying Well*. They hold that "a pattern of physical or psychological abuse of the spouse or the children effectively breaks the love commitment." They note that while the Catholic church historically has allowed no alternative but for the battered woman to continue in a marriage, "arguing that the evil of divorce was greater than the impact of violence or a loveless marriage on the spouse," today a

> clearer understanding of the destructiveness of such a marriage has made us aware of those situations in which a person may have a

moral obligation to divorce. Many Catholic theologians and ministers argue that other good outweighs the good of such a marriage
commitment and that fidelity as a Christian virtue extends to more
than the marriage bond. Fidelity to oneself and to one's children
may require ending such a marriage.[4]
Lewis Smedes offers a similar perspective: "Fidelity is a dynamic, positive posture that needs renewing and recreating constantly. It is not
achieved simply by staying out of other people's beds." Instead, fidelity
is a "person-keeping" commitment in which each partner in the marriage works at the "other's happiness, healing, wholeness and freedom." Under such a standard anything which violates a marriage
would be considered adultery. The seventh commandment addresses
violation of marriage by any means, Smedes charges.[5]

When reconciliation between spouses is no longer possible, as is
frequently the case in abusive marriages, Smedes asserts that "the
marriage is dead, and has no claim on us." This is not to minimize
the psychological or spiritual impact which this breach will have on
a victim, but rather is an acknowledgment of the right of the victim
to be released from a future of continued violence. A woman's decision
to no longer live under the threat of her husband's violence and with
the turmoil of a double life (externally pleasant, internally terrified)
may only be an admission of what actually exists, serving as a means
of making the abusive husband take responsibility for his violence.

Clearly God's intent from creation was not divorce, but companion-
ship. Yet there will always exist the tension of God's intent and people's sinful choices. And when a marriage is being suffocated by violence, threats and intimidation, the "law of love (agape) dictates that
there should be divorce," charges Richard Foster.[6] In such marriages
the perpetuation of abuse is far more damaging and sinful than is the
decision to divorce, he claims. And the burden should not be placed
on the victim to justify her actions but on the abuser to confess his
sin and demonstrate that destructive patterns have changed.

Foster goes on to illustrate the incredible risk of not submitting to this law of love. "If a woman comes in telling of marital rape and every other conceivable inhumanity, she is simply and grandly told that unless there is adultery or desertion she has no 'biblical' basis for divorce." Such a mentality, Foster declares, is an attempt to "turn the words of Jesus and Paul into a new legalism" that subtly reinforces the view that men are to remain dominant.[7]

Ethicist Allen Verhey analyzes the New Testament sayings with respect to marriage and divorce and asserts that we are not to understand the words of Jesus as a rigid moral rule but as "an invitation or a permission to share in the freedom Jesus gives to live marriage as God intended and intends."[8] Both preserving the external semblance of a marriage without the inner reality of marriage as God intended it to be and rigidly condemning divorce can be traced to moral pride, he continues. Rather than giving us specific legal requirements regarding marriage, God has called us

> to honor marriage as part of his intention for the creation. . . . Marriage is to be protected and honored—and marriage partners are to be protected and honored, loved and cherished. Divorce is always, therefore, an evil; it is never something to be intended as itself the end-in-view. But divorce is sometimes necessary 'between the times' for the protection and honoring of marriage itself or of one of the partners in marriage. As killing is sometimes allowable with fear and trembling, as in a just war, so divorce may sometimes be permissibly done accompanied by mourning and repentance.[9]

Far too many battered women have been told that in response to their submission God will either stop the violence or, as an equally acceptable solution, give them the endurance to live with that violence. Thus the expectation is that a wife should submit to her husband regardless of whether the abuse continues, since her responsibility is first and foremost to be submissive; her safety and right not to be violated are secondary to that spiritual responsibility. To endorse such a view of submission is to distort the biblical intent of submission and to pervert God's intention for the marriage relationship.

Jesus' words on marriage and divorce have been abstracted into a new "law of marriage and divorce," notes Ray Anderson, and the unfortunate result is that pastors use this as their framework for making decisions about how they will minister to those with

> marriages complicated by a web of casuistry involving hermeneutical hairsplitting in handling the biblical texts. Rather than being accountable to God himself, ministers often take refuge in abstract principles which either excuse them from acting on behalf of those who are in need of support when going through the breakdown of a marriage, or free them to act in every case with little regard for the implications of their actions. In either case, the commandment of God becomes trivialized and rendered ineffective.[10]

The Lessons from Real Life

To identify with a victim's pain and yet seriously interact with God's Word as it applies to the problem of divorce is a difficult task. Focusing on one appears to be at the peril of the other. What once was crystal clear appears to be opaque when you start applying Scripture to the lives of real people with real problems. For how God's Word applies to the real stuff of life can never be prescribed in a detached manner; it must come through personal interaction with individuals in pain and distress. Such a process must not rely exclusively on either personal experience or hermeneutical method but must become a wedding of the two.

A forum with four pastors on divorce and remarriage in *Leadership Journal* illustrates this principle well. In it one pastor stated that "if you're committed to marriage, there are no outs," yet later acknowledged, "I'll admit I've counseled women to separate—if their husbands were physically abusing them. I think self-preservation is biblical, an instinct God has given."[11] This pastor capitulates on his "marriage is

for keeps" theological perspective (for if he is honest, he will acknowledge that in many abusive marriages separation is merely a precursor
to divorce because so many abusers refuse treatment) not because of
what Scripture says but because he has reasoned that self-preservation
is a God-given instinct. His position has likely been informed by the
pain, terror and struggle of real victims. Such information requires the
pastor either to sensitively apply the Bible in a new light or to ignore
a victim's plight altogether.

In the same article Robert Wise, pastor of a Reformed Church in
America congregation in Oklahoma City, pointed out that he has seen
what he called the "daddy's daughter syndrome" at work with pastors.
It "doesn't matter what your theology of divorce is, it will change if
your daughter gets divorced," he contends. "In my denomination,
within a twelve-month period, six daughters of top-echelon leaders got
divorces, and suddenly policies were reconsidered. . . . With a daughter, daddies suddenly identify with the problem." Wise continued:

> I don't mean their revisions are self-serving. One man said to me,
> "For thirty years of ministry I had Matthew 19 down to a T, and
> then my daughter got divorced. I sat in my study for days and cried,
> remembering what I'd said to hundreds of people over the years.
> Those faces kept coming back to me, and I couldn't help thinking,
> My God, what will I do if somebody says all those things to my
> daughter?"[12]

While the application of Scripture can never be isolated from the
experiences of life, this is often an unacknowledged reality when it
comes to sensitive issues like marriage and divorce. Without doubt it
will be actual contact with battered women which will have the most
profound impact on the theological positions which pastors and denominations hold on this issue. Nonetheless, keeping a woman locked
into an abusive marriage through rigid doctrines and counsel can in
itself be an act of violence, a subtle form of collusion with evil.

Reconciliation would be a lot easier if it weren't for the people involved.

Lynn Buzzard[1]

———————

Therefore, if anyone is in Christ, he is a new creation; the old has gone,
the new has come! All this is from God, who reconciled us to
himself through Christ and gave us the ministry of reconciliation: that
God was reconciling the world to himself in Christ, not counting
men's sins against them. And he has committed to us
the message of reconciliation.

2 Corinthians 5:17-19

———————

9
The Church
and
Reconciliation

s an eight-year-old Alice was sexually abused by her brother in a hayloft. Forty years later as she talked about that incident and the many which followed, she spoke through tears. "I passed out and when I came to I was lying like I was hung on a cross. I carried that burden myself, thinking it was my own fault because of what I heard at church. The church was so powerful. The little girls sat down in front practically beneath the pulpit and the pastor always talked about hell, fire and brimstone, about harlots and adulterers. It always was the woman's fault. I wished then that I'd been born a boy. They seemed to be favored. They had a chance to go to high school. I didn't. My folks had insurance policies for my brothers. But not for the girls.

"When my brother was after me, I'd want to open the bedroom door and tell someone, but I couldn't. After I left home I finally realized why: My folks wouldn't have believed me. My brother was kingpin. I guess I would rather go on believing that they loved me than find out the truth."

Five weeks after marriage, her husband's emotional and sexual abusiveness started. "Being in control was so important to him. He would make comments about needing to break me like a horse. He didn't want his family to think he wasn't in control. I felt like I was in prison, like a caged bird. A bird who could fly but wasn't allowed."

Alice blames the bulk of her husband's problems on the strict religious environment in which they both were raised. "It caused the problems in the first place. There was no expressing of emotions, especially for men. The church gave him the right to do everything he did. All we ever heard was that the woman has to be submissive. It never taught the next thing, that the husband is to love his wife as his own body. I never heard those verses in church. I didn't even know they were in the Bible until I read them at home myself."

In recent years, the battered woman has had to be her own advocate in order to make her case known: she has left home, divorced her husband, set up shelters, written books, formed "radical" groups, marched on Washington, D.C. And like the persistent widow in Luke 18 who gets justice out of an evil judge because she doesn't give up, the battered woman has seen her persistence pay off.

Washington was the first state to respond to such persistence by enacting the Domestic Violence Act, recognizing domestic violence as a serious crime against society and assuring its victims maximum legal protection. Many other states have followed suit.

In Duluth, Minnesota, a year and a half after a program of compulsory arrests for batterers was established, the arrest, conviction and treatment of batterers was up by 400 per cent. Other cities are following Duluth's model, having realized that such imminent legal intervention is the most effective strategy for stopping wife abuse.

Through the now increasingly accepted approach of compulsory arrests, in many states a batterer can be arrested, convicted and treated without relying solely on the victim to press charges. If police receive a report of spouse battering, find physical injury and locate the abuser within four hours, they are required to arrest him whether or not the woman decides to press charges. They must also notify a women's shelter, which will send a counselor that same night to visit the man in jail and the victim at home, intending to follow the case through the legal process and expedite treatment.

If, like the evil judge who eventually responds with justice, an unredeemed society will hear the plight of the abused woman, can the people of God do any less? The prophet Jeremiah declares that to know Yahweh is to uphold justice for the oppressed (Jer 22:13-16). Throughout the Old Testament a knowledge of God is frequently demonstrated by a commitment to justice and compassion for the needy (Is 1:11-17; 42:5-7; Jer 9:23).

As long as the church is quiet in a world which resonates with the cries of abused women, it is failing in its ministry of reconciliation. It is simply functioning as sounding brass, a clanging cymbal. To fulfill its calling the church must "authenticate by acts which make for reconciliation the message of reconciliation which [it] proclaim[s]."[2]

The church is called to bind up the bruises of women who have suffered not only from the violence of their spouses, but also from the passive violence of a church which has failed to recognize their situation and intervene on their behalf. It is a call for the body of Christ to be broken bread and poured-out wine for victims: to serve them, nourish them and struggle along with them.

Few of the many victims we interviewed see the church as a positive agent of change in their situation; it has not actively worked for their protection or addressed their husbands' abusiveness with a balance of love and justice. Only a handful report that their churches have called "the wicked and evil man . . . to account for his wickedness" (Ps 10:15).

A commitment to an authentic ministry of reconciliation is a radical one indeed. Rather than being tidy and safe, it could more realistically be described as "a convoluted and obscure process which often becomes an emotional roller coaster for peacemakers," says Lynn Buzzard. "Like the model of Christ, the one who seeks to reconcile must become in some way incarnate and flesh out the painful realities of the human condition in order to invite it to renewal. No mere role of convener, discussion processor, collector of truth and formalizer of agreement seems sufficient to break through. It is often the mediator who takes the first risk, who first models vulnerability, confession and release."[3]

Love Which Takes Sides
If the problem of wife abuse is one of evil, the church can no longer avoid taking sides. "A love which intends to be effective in terms of God's kingdom cannot avoid taking sides," says theologian Jose Bonino.[4] In fact, the church will be in collusion with evil if it does not stand on the side of the victim. Only when it becomes an advocate for the oppressed can it fulfill its prophetic role.

But the church must be an advocate for the powerless not primarily because it has been catapulted into social action by a feminist critique on the treatment of women or because psychological research documents the victimization of women as fact. Instead, the church must aggressively respond because the presence of evil is revealed.

If the church is to be truly *pro-life,* how can it help but champion the cause of battered women? Being pro-life requires more than opposing abortion; it means taking a stance against all which stifles life and personhood. To be pro-life is to be *for* life. And violence by a husband toward his wife is one obvious offense to the integrity of human life. The life of any individual cannot be sustained—body, soul and spirit—

when it is destroyed by violence, domination, fear and threat.

Just as the prophets of the Old Testament "walked the streets of Israel's cities, probed into Judah's courts, poked around in the marketplaces, and were outraged at what they saw,"[5] so it is time for the church to become indignant when Christian marriages are soured by violence. "How is it," asks author Terry Davidson, "that decent, intelligent, law-abiding citizens act as though marital violence called for no outrage?"[6] The biblical standard of justice must be applied in these cases. And what does the Lord require of us? "To act justly and to love mercy and to walk humbly with your God" (Mic 6:8).

To break the bonds of injustice toward women, the church must accept its call to action. "Rescue those being led away to death; hold back those staggering toward slaughter," says Proverbs 24:11. These are active commands. The church cannot claim ignorance of the fact that wife abuse exists in its families and thus wash its hands of the matter. God will weigh the heart and "repay each person according to what he has done" (Prov 24:12). As Dietrich Bonhoeffer acknowledged, "Only he who believes is obedient, and only he who is obedient believes."[7] It is time for an obedience which acts.

Admitting That Wife Abuse Exists

Like any sin, wife abuse is no respecter of persons. It is not just "out there" in society; it flourishes within the confines of the body of Christ. By not acknowledging the problem, the church continues to suffer from a festering internal wound. And when it goes unchallenged, marital conflict of this magnitude prevents healthy family relationships and blocks effective ministry on every level. The church's silence on the subject—when it has been so vocal on issues such as prayer in the schools, homosexuality and abortion—is tacit permission for abuse to continue.

A woman from the Midwest, now leading a support group for abused women, noted that when she first told her pastor about being abused by her husband, the pastor said, "I'll never again bring this up." "I felt the message he gave me was 'Please don't bring this up. I don't want to deal with it.' Later, the pastor didn't even recall my having told him about the abuse. It scared him and he didn't listen." That woman subsequently left the marriage, that church and the evangelical denomination to which she had belonged since her youth. "Part of the problem was that I didn't feel the church was going to support me. I felt that I couldn't be a good Christian and get out of my home environment. It kept me in a sick, abusive marriage for twenty-one years."

How can the church communicate its willingness to support the battered woman and her husband? By talking about this taboo subject in prayers, sermons and Sunday-school lessons. One former victim, now heading a task force for battered women in her rural area, tells pastors in the ministerial associations she addresses to pray at the end of each service for "homes where there is violence, homes where women and children are abused. It gets the church familiar with the words 'battered woman' so they aren't so afraid of them. And it lets the battered woman in the congregation know that the pastor is aware of the problem. She'll think, 'He does care about me. I can go talk to him.' "

Announcements can be made from the pulpit about area shelters or support groups for abusers and victims. The problem can also be discussed in Sunday-school classes or confronted directly in a sermon on the subject of family violence. These small steps help raise the level of awareness of the issue in the congregation and may be the impetus for a practical ministry to abused women and their families.

Seeing the Signs
Awareness of the problem is the first step forward for the church. The second is having the compassion to look for the telltale signs of abuse among other churchgoers.

For example, several women advised pastors to be wary of couples who are "too good to be true." Chances are that they simply aren't *true.* Said one wife: "I knew that if I didn't treat him well and act real happy in public, I'd get it at home." Frequent church hopping, intermittent attendance and inappropriate outbursts of anger by the husband can also be signals.

Another sign to look for are very "private" couples, those who keep to themselves and rarely socialize or interact individually with church friends or even relatives. Often one of the abuser's first ploys is systematically breaking down any network of outside contacts his wife or children may seek to develop. Limits are placed on phone calls and visits with close family members. The abusive husband is jealous of his wife's friendships because they threaten his ability to wield control over her actions and opinions. Hence, she may be prohibited from entertaining others in the home. And even if the children are permitted to have friends over, they frequently choose not to do so because of the tension involved.

The loneliness and isolation are not limited to the wife and children, of course. The batterer himself is an island, cut off from friendship and intimacy. "A Christian man to have befriended my husband would have been a blessing and a relief to us all," reported a woman from England.[8]

A Look Inward

If it is to have a significant impact in the area of wife beating, the church must not focus solely on how to help or "treat" the battered woman. Examination also needs to be given to the type of religious environment which permits the abuse of women to occur without reparations.

Bishop Desmond Tutu, relating the indignities to which all Blacks in South Africa are subjected—house searches in the middle of the night, strip searches at roadside tents, armored tanks rumbling through the streets—charged that the ultimate blasphemy of such a situation is that it makes "a child of God doubt that he or she is a child of God. The authorities are intent not only on rubbing your human dignity in the dust, but, having done so, they trample it underfoot."[9]

Such crazy-making circumstances are not unlike the humiliating world in which the battered woman lives. Consequently, when she musters up the courage to go public with "her" problem (very likely first to her pastor or a church member), what little human dignity she has retained can soon be "trampled underfoot" with comments like: "What have you done to provoke him?" "Well, you've got to understand that your husband is under a lot of pressure right now," or "How would Jesus want you to act? Just submit and it won't happen again."

A much more constructive approach would be for a pastor to "preach a sermon verifying that Christ did not endorse wife beating and neither does he," suggests author Terry Davidson, whose father was a minister and an abuser. "Speak out from the pulpit and face the fact that wife beating is sinful. And when a battered wife comes to you, don't exclude her husband from your pastoral counseling."[10]

Acknowledging Abuse as Sin

One giant step toward rebuilding the shattered self-esteem of Christian battered women would be made if the church acknowledged that wife abuse is a sin. Wife abuse *is* sin, and the psalmist is unequivocal in stating so.

> Therefore pride is their necklace; they clothe themselves with violence. From their callous hearts comes iniquity; the evil conceits of their minds know no limits. They scoff, and speak with malice; in their arrogance they threaten oppression. Their mouths lay claim to heaven, and their tongues take possession of the earth. (Ps 73:6-9)

To recognize abuse as sin will often require the appropriation of church discipline. Numerous battered women with whom we talked noted that their violent husbands were not dismissed from the church board, refused Communion or released from teaching Sunday-school class even after their abuse became known to the pastor, despite the biblical standards of conduct for those in leadership. First Timothy 3:3 states that a person setting his heart on leadership must not be "violent but gentle," clearly excluding the one who is abusive. The women, meanwhile, report being rejected or disciplined by the church for pursuing separation or divorce because of their husband's violence.

On one level, such a stance is understandable. Battered women are often depressed, anxiety-ridden, suffering from low self-esteem or displaying a countenance of helplessness. Some have attempted suicide; others have abused drugs or been sexually promiscuous. Such appearances have provided ample justification for rejecting the complaints of victims and ignoring their cries for help. It is not uncommon for doctors to prescribe mood-elevating drugs for a victim of abuse when she alludes to the violence in her home. Many an abuser has, under the guise of concern, taken his wife to talk with the pastor who, in turn, becomes an unwitting participant in the husband's scheme to uncover her "insecurities." And more than one victim has had her husband attempt to have her committed to a psychiatric ward.

Ministering to the needs of the abused wife means not only a willingness to stand in the gap by providing for physical services such as child care or temporary housing but also a commitment to the long-term process of rebuilding the dignity of a woman whose sense of worth has been shattered. It is the Christian community's responsibility to restore the dignity which the battered woman has lost due in part to the church's questioning of her credibility, sanity or even her right to object to mistreatment.

A Complex Problem

Working with abused women requires a willingness to struggle not only with theological and spiritual issues, but with complex psychological ones as well. A pastor can expect that efforts to intervene in the life of a battered woman will be characterized by trial separations, emotional vacillation and the full range of possible disappointments. Researchers Hilberman and Munson note that their work with sixty victims was "slow, frustrating and intensely anxiety-provoking," and they challenge the treatment person to keep two realities in mind: the client's progress is usually very slow—even inconsequential at first— and the course of treatment is often stormy and unpredictable. Both dynamics can easily drain the therapist.[11]

Why is working with abused women so difficult? First, the physical danger a woman experiences places her in need of numerous resources (shelter, emotional support, financial support and so on), while the availability of these resources is limited. Second, the victim often has mixed feelings about getting help. This ambivalence may regress into a fatalistic view of herself and her future.

The third factor is the actual physical danger which exists for those who work with victims of abuse. The possibility that the abuser will attempt to intimidate the pastor, therapist or friend is very real. The abusive husband of one woman unexpectedly interrupted her therapy session by shouting accusations at the therapist and roughly pushing him into a chair. The therapist's response at that point was critical. "It was vital not to further exacerbate the man and yet to firmly communicate that his behavior was unacceptable," he recalled. "I told him that he would have to sit down if he were going to stay and that if he was ever assaultive again, either during our session or toward his wife, he would be arrested. Often that's the only thing the batterer hears."

Working with battered women is also difficult for pastors because they are often uncomfortable with the topic. The avoidance of issues like wife abuse by ministers, contends one Minneapolis pastor, is root- ed in the theological training they receive. He reported that most of his seminary training had to do with managing "either the church community or theology. By and large, we pastors have not been trained to open ourselves to people. For me to help someone in an abuse situation is to take a step *out* of control. Pastors tend to defend themselves from dealing with people. They *manage* people. To confront domestic abuse is to confront the failure of the church. It brings two very direct indictments against the church: How do we deal with our own guilt and with the fact that this problem exists in our own flock? Pastors very often find themselves floundering theologically when confronted with a battered woman."

Personal Discomfort

Research indicates that personal discomfort with a topic as volatile and close to home as wife abuse is a key reason it was ignored by the psychological community and society in general until the early 1970s.[12] And, as sociologists William Stacey and Anson Shupe point out in *The Family Secret,* the clergy are no exception among those who have been slow to recognize the serious and widespread nature of family violence. "Learning to counsel families with this problem is not a regular part of seminary training," they note. "Courses in pastoral counseling do not normally deal with assault, incest and rape."[13]

A 1986 survey of clergy counseling activities in south-central Connecticut revealed that most clergy "had not received formal training in counseling," yet all had experience with "troubled individuals." "Marriage, family and psychological problems were those most frequently brought to the clergy; fewer than ten per cent of the counseling problems were spiritual in nature." Nonetheless, the study found, these clergy members referred "less than ten per cent of their counselees to specialized mental-health resources. . . . Evangelical clergy were the most self-contained group, making and receiving few referrals except from other clergy."[14]

Few pastors possess the counseling skills, knowledge of local laws or awareness of social resources required to effectively deal with abused women. An Illinois woman who counseled with three pastors noted, "Pastors need to realize that 'normal' marriage counseling isn't going to do the trick. Because of sin and lack of inner healing, there are going to be marriages that don't go by the books."

Furthermore, on a personal level pastors are not likely to be emotionally prepared to handle the feelings of outrage which this issue will raise. In light of the intense range of feelings ignited within the counselor by this problem, the often unpredictable time demands made by victims of such abuse, and the fact that professionally trained counselors consistently report a need for specialized training in order to work with these women, the pastor would need a thorough awareness of his own feelings and reactions in order to offer effective counsel to abused women.

Interestingly enough, fifty-eight per cent of the pastors who participated in a 1983 survey of 266 pastors said they did not experience difficulty in counseling battered women and regarded themselves as competent to perform the task.[15] The majority of the abused women seen by these pastors were reported to have had sexual problems, health complications due to the violence or considered suicide, conditions all linked to the abuse. And a substantial number (forty-one per cent) had previously seen a counselor regarding the problem of marital violence and had used drugs in response to it. Any one of these problems could in and of itself require a well-trained counselor, but a combination thereof often results in a morass of problems requiring a level of psychological training that most pastors simply do not have.

The fact that only one-third of the pastors found the emotional demands made by these women difficult to handle may indicate that these pastors misperceived their preparedness as counselors or minimized the personal struggles involved in counseling abuse victims. They simply may have been out of touch with the pain of the victims.

What emerges from this data is a picture of the pastor as someone with extraordinary confidence in his own abilities, a view consistent

with the conclusions reached by the National Association of Evangelicals Task Force on the Family in 1985. The NAE study characterized
the evangelical pastor as a

> lonely person in matters of competence and security in assisting
> family development in their congregations. Almost half of those
> surveyed have never or only once attended any sort of workshop or
> program of assistance related to their skills in dealing with family
> matters. Half of the respondents indicate never having turned to
> another pastor for help with family concerns in their congregations.
> Almost half say that they have never helped another pastor in such
> matters. At the same time a strong evidence emerged in the "com-
> ments" section of the questionnaire concerning distrust of counsel-
> ors outside the church. One must wonder to whom the majority
> of these pastors can turn for professional assistance in matters of
> family development and need for therapeutic assistance.[16]

Though pastors may appear to be lonely, they present themselves to
be a "rather secure and even self-confident set of human beings" who
"judge their own level of competence to help other people with family
concerns as being relatively high."

Unfortunately, such a misplaced confidence may be a major reason
that the church's attempts to minister to abusive families have been
largely ineffective. The clergy's track record won't improve until pastors acknowledge their limitations and willingly seek help from other
professionals.

Redefining the Role of "Roles"
The history of the divine right of husbands to punish or administer
"lawful correction" to their wives permeates both legal and church
history. Until the late nineteenth century all of the "legal systems of
Europe, England and early America supported a husband's right to beat
his wife and so did the community norms." In this country, prior to
1870 a husband could legally go unpunished for "beating [his wife]

with a stick, pulling her hair, choking her, spitting in her face, kicking her about the floor."[17] While many historical church documents omit discussion of a husband's chastisement of his wife, there is some evidence that physical abuse of women was even recommended by both pastors and theologians.[18] By the Middle Ages the status of women in the Roman Catholic Church was so low that one writer records that men were "exhorted from the pulpit to beat their wives and wives to kiss the rod that beat them."[19]

Appalled by the casualness with which Christian lords and princes murdered their wives, the Abbé de Brontome stated in the fourteenth century, "To think that the pagans of old, who did not know Christ, were so gentle and kind to their wives; and that the [majority] of our lords should be so cruel to them."[20]

Such a heritage is not a biblical one. But it nonetheless has been influential. It is a shackle from which we have yet to be freed. Within conservative evangelical circles the entire issue of roles has been elevated to a level of idolatry. Definitions are very authoritatively given as to just what a woman's role or a man's role is to be, without any sensitivity as to how culturally determined those interpretations are or without any regard for the variety of gifts God has freely given irrespective of sex. Women don't speak up in services lest they be considered "out of order," while men proclaim scriptural justification for their assuming leadership in everything from preaching and teaching to balancing the checkbook. The notion of man as "head of the home" is repeated so often that one can scarcely recall that the phrase is found nowhere in the Bible.

Ben Kinchlow, former "700 Club" cohost, said in a magazine interview:

In every place where you find a woman in charge, you find a weak man. Men were designed to be the head of the family. If you are reading this . . . and the husband is not head of the family, without even talking to you, I can guarantee that you have financial problems, marital problems, and perhaps emotional problems with your children.[21]

Such a view, charges author Gretchen Gaebelein Hull, "contradicts the many Scripture passages where God's Word teaches that *both* parents share responsibility for the family."[22]

A Preventive Approach

Education within the church about the problem of wife abuse must be preventative in nature if it is to touch the issue at its root. So endemic is violence to family life that in an astonishingly high number of cases, violence is evident prior to marriage. A study of 296 California high-school students found that about twenty-seven per cent of those surveyed had experienced some form of violence while dating. The violence occurred "irrespective of race, religion, economic level, grade or academic standing," said Esther Chew, coauthor of the study.[23]

Likewise, in 1981, sociologist James Makepeace questioned 202 students at St. John's University and found that 21.2 per cent had experienced some form of violence in a dating relationship. Expanding that study to include college students from seven midwestern and western colleges, Makepeace and two other researchers determined that 16.8 per cent of their sample had suffered at least one incident of violence during courtship. Twice as many women as men had experienced dating violence. And the violence, which often started during high school, generally began with an argument over jealousy or sex; for twenty per cent it involved an attempt at forced sex.

"We don't teach our young men and women to communicate honestly in dating," suggests Bev Wesley, one of the sociologists conducting the study. "Despite all the clamor and headlines about changing sex roles, young women still learn to be cute, sexually attractive, flirtatious and submissive in a dating relationship. . . . They aren't supposed to take responsibility or control. The young man, meanwhile, still learns to play the aggressor."[24]

A similar study of 485 randomly selected college students revealed that a startling 40.5 per cent had experienced some sort of violence during their courtships. Men were twice as likely as women to perceive those violent acts as improving the relationship. Sociologist John Murphy states, "Basically, courtship violence is about power. The issue of courtship violence is one which has been ignored for too long."[25]

A preventative program needs to be directed to youth as they form their attitudes toward the structure of male-female relationships—who makes decisions, how they are made, what "rights" they have within relationships, what is "allowed" by each sex within a relationship. It should include expanding content within Sunday-school classes to patterns of communication within male-female relationships, conflict resolution and challenging kids to define what their assumptions are about male-female interaction.

In particular, girls need to be encouraged to trust themselves in their decisions and to value their own perceptions. All too often, battered women report having had an uneasiness about their spouse before marriage but felt pressured to dismiss such fears. Instead these concerns and fears should be brought out and directly addressed.

Blinded by Bias

We believe that one of the primary reasons so little serious attention has been given to the problem of wife abuse, both from a biblical perspective (for there is much within Scripture which directly addresses this problem) and from a psychological one, is that it has been men who were the writers, preachers, counselors, interpreters of the Word and authorities on family life. The selective inattention to this problem within the Christian world may reveal the inability of many men in leadership positions, accustomed to viewing life from a position of power and control, to remove the blinders of bias they wear and actually see what life looks like from the bottom side up.

It is the same principle at work that writers Berkeley and Alvera

Mickelsen have noted in their research into how male dominance has tarnished the translation of Scripture itself.

We doubt if any of the men on translation committees or who did their own translations are conscious of any male chauvinism. All are honest, godly scholars, dedicated to doing their best work, trying faithfully to bring to today's readers the message of the Bible.

But like all of us, these translators grew up in a society that assumed males should dominate home, church, and society at large. It has been as much a part of our culture (and of most pagan cultures) as the air we breathe. Translators naturally tend to read and interpret the Bible from the framework in which they have lived and thought.[26]

Thus, as the Mickelsens point out, the word *head* in 1 Corinthians 11:3 is rendered "supreme over" (TEV); *deacon* in relationship to Phoebe in Romans 16:1 is translated "servant" (KJV); and all the one-man translations of 1 Corinthians 11:10 (Taylor, Phillips, Bratcher) "added man or husband to this passage despite the fact that Paul says nothing about a man or a husband."[27]

A Warning to Shepherds

The words of the prophet Ezekiel to the "shepherds of Israel" apply to many leaders of the church today. It is a warning to those who have been appointed to "take care of the flock" and who have failed in their responsibilities. Ezekiel does not mince words: "You have not strengthened the weak or healed the sick or bound up the injured. . . . You have ruled them harshly and brutally" (Ezek 34:4). And, because of such harsh rule, because of the dismissal of the plight and pain of the sheep, because of the complicity of the shepherds with evil, "I am against the shepherds and will hold them accountable for my flock. I will remove them from tending the flock" (v. 10).

It has been men who have decided, until at least very recently, what Scripture has to say about marriage and how a woman should respond to an abusive husband. It has been men who have judged the pain of these women and generally found it insufficient to justify marital separation, legal action or divorce. It has been men who have ignored or dismissed this brutality against women. Men have failed to communicate God's compassion toward these victims of oppression.

Again, prophetic words from South Africa have much relevancy with regard to the plight of battered women:

It is tragic when hierarchical religiosity in its detached "piety," pontificating in ontological distance from the human trauma and tragedy . . . can ignore the root causes for the bitterness and the unrest of a desperate people. We have no right to come as Job's comforters with slick analyses and ideological labels, while showing no concern for the dilemma of Job's misery and human complaint.[28]

The word of hope to battered women, then, is found in God's promise that he will bless them and they will be "secure in their land."

I will send down showers in season; there will be showers of blessing. . . . They will know that I am the LORD, when I break the bars of their yoke and rescue them from the hands of those who enslaved them. . . . They will live in safety, and no one will make them afraid. (Ezek 34:26-28)

Like the Reverend Martin Luther King, Jr., we too have a dream. We dream of a time when Christian women and children will be safe in their homes, when they will no longer fear being left unprotected by society and the community of believers. Ours is a dream of the Christian world as a place where both women and men will be affirmed as equal heirs before Christ, where both women and men will be free to use their God-given gifts to his glory. We have a dream of a day that Isaiah foretold: "No longer will violence be heard in your land, nor ruin or destruction within your borders, but you will call your walls Salvation and your gates Praise" (Is 60:18).

After attending your first Sunday school class . . . I felt as though someone cracked the door to a huge, ugly pit in my life. But there was something that felt wonderful about it . . . to think that, maybe, there was someone who knew what I knew—that within the church, families were dying and that they were all alone. . . . The pain and the fear and the doubt are all still there, but now I feel that I've given myself permission to believe again—a little bit.

The walls of the compartments in my life are getting lower. I hope that sometime they will be gone. The thought of experiencing health intrigues me. That's what I want for myself and my family. I'm willing to look at what it may cost. And I'm hoping that I can accept what that affords, . . . trying to believe that I deserve it. I want to thank you both for "going out on a limb" and for being there for me. I'm going to make it.

From a battered woman who attended a Sunday-school class on conflict in marriage

---

Conclusion:
Violence
in the
Land

Violence of one sort or another is a fact of twentieth-century American life. It is as American as apple pie. And it is as entrenched in family life as it is within the history of our country. Idealized as a "cradle of comfort," the home is more realistically a hotbed of violence, according to a 1978 National Crime Survey which labelled the home, at night, the most dangerous place to be and the most likely setting for homicide to occur.

A report by the National Commission on the Causes and Prevention of Violence stated that eighteen per cent of the adults sampled acknowledged having slapped or kicked another person, while thirteen per cent had been slapped or kicked as adults. FBI statistics verify that twenty-five per cent of the 4,660 murders committed in the United

States in 1975 occurred within the family, and over half took place in the context of a husband-wife argument. Those figures average out to about four spouses a day slain by their partners. They do not take into consideration the hundreds of spouses who are brutally attacked—though not murdered—each day.

Ours is undeniably a violent culture, one which not only accepts but often glorifies violence through television and movie heroes. While the image of the brooding, silent male who woos and wins the beautiful, classy woman has long been a Hollywood staple, a disturbing change has taken place in the characterization of male heroes, as Los Angeles writer Joyce Sunila notes.

In the last 10 years, the menacing male's inner temperature has risen. The '70s saw the emergence of a new breed of menace, the amphetamine-crazed brooder, a la Jack Nicholson, Robert De Niro and Al Pacino. Suddenly we had guys who twitched all over the screen and could explode at any moment over something like somebody ordering the wrong flavor ice cream. Often they were openly abusive toward women, particularly in such Martin Scorsese movies as "New York, New York" and "Raging Bull." From the stoicism of a Bogart, we entered a world where male menace no longer was potential. It was real and present. These guys would haul off and belt you![1]

In her article "Images of Violence against Women," Julia London identifies the sexism and blatant hostility which underlie many socially held attitudes toward women as manifested through the media.

A New York City fashion photographer recently told *Time* magazine: "The violence is in the culture, so why shouldn't it be in our picture?" *Vogue,* for instance, published a twelve-page spread by Richard Avedon showing a man alternately caressing and menacing a female model. At the dramatic peak of the sequence, the man smashes the woman across the face. . . . Pictures like these glorify the cruel, painful reality of violence against women and support the

myths and stereotypes that accompany its justification.[2]
The image of woman as an appropriate recipient of violence is a pervasive message which ultimately minimizes—if not encourages—the
seriousness of wife abuse. That is not to imply, however, that family
violence is the result of external pressures alone. While media violence
may exacerbate the problem of wife abuse, it does not cause it. A search
for the causes of wife abuse leads back to the family itself.

Beyond Myths

In her book *Friends As Family,* author Karen Lindsey challenges the
oft-touted theme "that if people would only stop worrying about their
own personal fulfillment and return to the loving bosom of the patriarchal family, the world would be a happy place."[3] The perspective that
what we need is a return to the good old days before the breakdown
of the nuclear family is a myth, she charges. It ignores the issue of
intrafamily abuse which has always been a reality. "When *was* the
Golden Age of the happy family?" she asks, chronicling the abuses
against women and children throughout history.

But we have lived with the myth of family and married life as a haven
of comfort and nurture for so long that to consider an alternative is
appalling and viewed as an attack on our Christian faith. We are of-
fended by reports which contradict our views; they require a total
structural shift in our understanding of marriage. They personally challenge us to examine what is perhaps most basic to our identity as
human beings: our sense of membership in a family.

Sociologists William Stacey and Anson Shupe counter the perspective of spokespersons for the New Christian Right, such as Jerry Falwell
and Phyllis Schlafly:

This is the myth of family violence: that it is a product of forces
and pressures coming from outside the family. We need not dwell
on the sexist nature of such myths. However, the point is that by
focusing attention on things outside the family, "analysts" like

Falwell undoubtedly miss one of the most pervasive, destructive forces threatening it. This force does not arise from without but rather from within the family. Violence is the real threat to the American family, and it is generated among family members. It can be found among couples where one or both persons lack honest, effective communication skills and ways to control anger and frustration. It can be found in the still-prevalent traditional attitudes among men that violence is an acceptable means of settling marital disputes and that as heads of the household they essentially hold property rights over women and children.[4]

Such attitudes can also be found Christian homes. Christians are right in their assessment that the family is under attack. But they've often failed to accurately discern where that attack is coming from.

Traditionally, the abuse of women has been denied or ignored by the church. It has aligned itself with the *status quo* and preached patriarchy as a God-ordained social order. But the Christian community must no longer avoid this problem, whether overtly or latently manifested. It must initiate radical change, first by admitting that the cancer of wife abuse does indeed exist in its homes and then by responding with concrete love and action to both victims and perpetrators. The church must also re-examine longstanding theological interpretations which have fueled the flames of oppression of women.

Questioning Traditions
It is evident from the bulk of what is written and preached by evangelicals today that most pastors hold patriarchal world views which they believe to be divinely ordained. In June 1984, for example, the 14.1 million-member Southern Baptist Convention passed a resolution which excluded women from pastoral leadership because "the man was first in creation and the woman first in the Edenic fall." This resolution clearly states that women are responsible for the Fall and that men are superior because they were created first.[5] The championing of such a

perspective requires that the church always hold in view a distinct (and essentially qualitative) difference between the sexes. Such an attitude, we believe, encourages Christians to minimize the problems of battered women and to respond reluctantly to their circumstances.

At the other extreme are those who reject the authority of Scripture because they have seen it used to justify the mistreatment of women. Writer and consultant to the American Baptist Churches' Task Force on Battered Women, Terry Davidson sees Scripture as a "literary work" which developed a "creation myth" that incorporated a "snake story."[6] Arguing that Christianity maintained an early contempt for women which arose out of man's own sexual weakness and conflicted with the ideal celibate life, she suggests that the Adam and Eve account is a "twisted" rationalization for the Christian world's abuse of women.[7] To someone like Davidson, the Southern Baptist resolution would be ample evidence that abuse is still rampant today.

It is our desire to strike a balance between these two extremes—the culturally biased literalistic reading of Scripture, which has too often resulted in a lack of concern for a battered woman and an insistence that she *make* the marriage work regardless of the obstacles, and the rejection of Scripture as merely an oppressive myth which eliminates the only real avenue for healing and reconciliation.

We recognize the validity of the feminist struggle over this issue and do not immediately reject their critiques; they have said much about this problem that Christians need to hear. Even a cursory look at church history reveals that women *have* suffered much at the hands of those who have taken the patriarchal view to radical extremes. Women, with few exceptions, have been subordinated. But we do not believe that secular feminists, with their blanket rejection of Scripture, have a foundation for building the bridge of reconciliation between the sexes. That bridge is Jesus Christ and, when the love of Jesus is free to work, it can transform not only individuals but marriage as well.

The limited research that has systematically investigated the relationship between wife abuse and religiosity indicates that physical abuse is less frequent in religious than in nonreligious homes. We accept those findings. But we are also concerned that Christians therefore not dismiss wife abuse as an issue of little importance within the Christian community.

Masked Violence

We further speculate that most often the violence that is brought against women in the Christian world is *not* physical. From what we have learned, the emotional abuse and manipulation of Christian women is far more frequent than their physical abuse. In fact, men who perceive their position before God as superior to that of women generally will not need to resort to physical violence. When a man can psychologically overpower his wife and justify his actions through a misapplication of Scripture, physical violence is less necessary. There are many ways to inflict violence, to violate what God has created. And the women with whom we have talked admit that their emotional mistreatment has often been as damaging as the physical abuse they have suffered.

Psychological abuse is "masked violence," contends marriage, family and child counselor Christine Buchholy from her work with victims of psychological abuse. She defines *masked violence* as a "subtle and repeated attack on one's sense of self as a valuable, intelligent human being, as well as an attack on one's sense of safety. One always fears, at least on an unconscious level, that psychological abuse may precipitate physical violence."[8]

Examining the close connection between power and fear, theologian Henri J. M. Nouwen notes, "Much power is exercised by instilling fear in people and keeping them afraid. Fear is one of the most effective weapons in the hands of those who seek to control us."[9] Such fear often permeates the internal framework which women in the church experience, often the result of the subtle but oppressive messages that they are "not quite good enough."

"Within a framework of inequality the existence of conflict is denied and the means to engage openly in conflict are excluded," contends psychiatrist Jean Baker-Miller.[10] Thus, inequality generates a hidden conflict for which "there are no acceptable social forms or guides because this conflict supposedly doesn't exist."[11] This denial of conflict is often evident in relationships between Christian couples who trust that adherence to biblical roles, which are rigidly defined, will eliminate any marital problems. The result is hidden conflict that is never honestly acknowledged and which often culminates in a destructive and violent outburst.

When through the misapplication of Scripture men dominate their wives, it is often a psychological tactic to avoid being honest about their own insecurities. A man may chide his wife for "not being submissive," but what he is really saying is, "I feel insecure when I'm not dominant and in charge." Such an unbiblical and psychologically unhealthy lust for power, rather than being challenged, is often tolerated in the Christian community and supported through scriptural prooftexting.

It is our contention that patriarchy is more an outgrowth of tradition and male pride than an accurate reflection of the whole counsel of Scripture. As such, it perpetuates a view of women that can result in their physical mistreatment. The roots of violence in any relationship lie in an unequal distribution of power. And a patriarchal system, however it is explained or rationalized, necessarily means that the dominant partner—the husband—has more power than his wife. To some degree, the Lucy Tisland story with which we began this book is the outcome of just such a distorted view taken to its logical conclusion.

Our focus has been on physical wife abuse. But that is only one form which the victimization of women can take. It is our hope that this book will help stimulate a re-examination of broader issues such as current attitudes toward women, marriage and the sanctity of person-hood within the Christian community.

This book is a call to justice, a plea for the church to put an end to the violence—both subtle and direct—that it has brought against women by not granting them the full status that is theirs as people created in the image of God. The body of Christ is suffering because it is at war with itself. Men need to be reconciled to women—redeemed from their disregard for them, their disparaging attitudes toward them, their sense of self-righteous superiority over them.

By sowing the seeds of patriarchy and hierarchy, we have reaped the fruit of divisiveness within the Christian home. We must heed Jesus' warning: "A house divided against itself will fall" (Lk 11:17).

Appendix:
The Response of
Clergy to the Problem
of Wife Abuse

The claim is made by some writers in the field of domestic violence that pastors hold a patriarchally informed attitude toward women which predisposes them to respond to victims of wife abuse in a distrustful, even subtly accusatory manner. In an effort to assess the validity of that claim, a questionnaire was sent to over 5,000 Protestant pastors throughout the United States to evaluate firsthand their experiences with the problem.[1]

The opinion that pastors do hold such views was partially confirmed in our study. However, the comments from pastors revealed them to be a group concerned about women but torn by the theological perspectives they hold which conflict with this concern.

In general, uncertainty about issues such as divorce and marital roles leads pastors to respond in a guarded manner and to minimize the abuse that battered women report to them. Furthermore, a substantial gap exists between the accounts pastors give and the negative reports of many victims about the pastoral advice they have received. The results of this study may reflect the need by pastors to provide socially acceptable answers, and appear compassionate and helpful, more than it reflects what they actually do and the counsel they give when dealing with abused women.

Pastors from all regions of the country were represented in the survey sample, and three denominations (Assemblies of God, Independent and Baptist-General Conference) accounted for almost one-third of the total respondents. The remaining two-thirds included pastors from thirty-one various Protestant denominations.

Since less than ten per cent of the questionnaires were returned, generalizations made from this survey are tentative and limited to pastors who did respond. Nonetheless, we venture that the information drawn from these pastors may well reflect a much larger percentage of evangelical Protestant pastors. What the response rate might be indicating, unfortunately, is the disinterest and even denial of the problems which many evangelical pastors have concerning the issue of wife abuse.

Four-fifths of the pastors in our sample indicated that they had confronted wife abuse in their ministry and counseled a woman who had been physically abused by her husband, and about one-third had counseled six or more such women. Three-fifths of the pastors had counseled a victim during the six months prior to completing the questionnaire, indicating that wife abuse is a problem with which pastors are currently dealing.

The profiles which the pastors provided of the women they had counseled indicate that the violence affected these women in serious ways. A majority of the women were from middle-class homes, had at least a high-school education, at least one child and held a part-time

job. Almost half had been Christians for over four years, married for
at least four years and experienced violence within the first three years
of marriage. The seriousness of their experiences with spousal abuse
was evident from the fact that over half were reported to have considered suicide, experienced health-related problems or had sexual problems within marriage. A third of the women were identified as having
used alcohol or other drugs to deal with the violence.

Is It Really a Problem?

Do pastors think that wife abuse is a problem in Christian homes? As
a group they did not dismiss it, nor did they suggest that Christians
are somehow immune to it. Sixty-three per cent estimated that it
occurs "sometimes," while twenty-eight per cent said that it occurs
less frequently than that; only eight per cent contended that it occurs
"often."

"This entire subject is dominant among believers," charged one
pastor from the South. "The tragedy is that churches don't care and
are ignorant about the subject." Another pastor anticipates its emergence as an issue within his community: "This is not a real concern
in our area *yet.*" And a pastor from the West cited a problem he had
faced in his counseling sessions. "Many women who come for counseling have been physically abused, but do not mention that fact for
many sessions, even years," he said. "When they do, they minimize the
incidents."

Finally, a pastor shared the pain he experienced in discovering, too
close to home, that wife abuse was indeed a problem in the church.
"My own daughter lived three years with a physically abusive husband,
who attended seminary. She had to leave him when her life was in
danger. She kept the abuse from us until she could take it no more."

Submission to Stop the Violence

Because the church has placed such emphasis on the submission of women to men and because researchers point to this emphasis as a primary precipitant to marital violence, pastors were asked if they agreed with the following statement: "If a woman submits to her husband as God desires, God will eventually honor her and either the abuse will stop or God will give her the strength to endure it." The majority of the pastors (seventy-three per cent) did not agree, and less than one-third of the respondents felt that the "unwillingness of some wives to be submissive to their husbands" accounted for their husbands' violence.

The fact, however, that more than one out of four pastors holds the belief that a wife, by submitting to her violent husband, can be assured that either the violence will stop or she will be able to endure it bolsters the claims of many victims that often pastors simply do not hear their pain. It indicates that such pastors, though a minority, trust a formula of submission by wives to their husbands, regardless of the circumstances of their pain.

For the twenty-seven per cent of the sample that felt that if a woman submits to her husband as God desires, God will eventually honor her and either the abuse will stop or God will give her the strength to endure it, to take such a stance is to acknowledge that the principle of wifely submission preempts other considerations, such as that of a woman's safety. This was evident by the fact that pastors who stressed wifely submission were also opposed to victims using certain protective legal and medical resources and were inclined to discount women's reports of violence.

Comments from a few pastors indicated that they had struggled with the issue of women's roles as it relates to marital violence. Said one, the church must rethink its theology and "dispel the rumor of woman's nonequality with men—from a biblical basis." Another contended that "treating women as second-class citizens has the effect of dehumanizing them—which allows a husband to mistreat his wife because she is not his equal."

Believing the Victim

A necessary precondition for helping abuse victims is to believe their reports of marital violence. While our study revealed that about only one of five pastors directly questioned a woman's report of the frequency and severity of the violence she had received and felt that "society, particularly the women's movement" had overestimated the problem of wife abuse, almost twice as many said that victims overestimate the batterer's responsibility for violence. Thus, fully a third of the pastors question the reliability of an abused woman's report when it comes to the issue of who is responsible for the violence.

Even more alarming was the finding that almost half of the pastors were concerned that the husband's violence not be overemphasized and used as a "justification" for breaking the marriage commitment. This pattern of responses suggests more of a willingness by pastors to believe women when they report how often they have been abused or how severe the violence has been than to believe the woman's assessment of who is responsible for the violence.

While it is difficult to know why this is so, the explanation may well go beyond the fact that "there are two sides to every story" and more accurately reflect a subtle blaming of the victim by pastors. Such reports are commonly voiced by victims. The number of pastors—one out of three—who mistrust women regarding the responsibility they assign their husbands raises our concern. Research consistently points to the fact that victims assume more—not less—responsibility for their husbands' violence. Consequently, many pastors may be heightening the destructive, self-blaming process already in motion.

Justification for Leaving

Much of the criticism leveled at pastors is that they minimize the severity of the violence reported by women because of their traditional attitudes toward marriage (in other words, maintain the marriage at all costs). Pastors were asked to rate just how intense marital violence would have to be in order to justify a Christian woman leaving the home. One-third of the respondents felt that the abuse would have to be life-threatening. Almost one-fifth believed that no amount of abuse would justify a woman leaving, while one in seven felt a moderate expression of violence would be justification enough. The remainder interpreted "occasional" violence as grounds for leaving.

The decision on the part of a pastor to support the dissolution of a marriage in order to end the violence reflects, in part, a commitment to the sanctity of personhood. So pastors were asked whether they would support a bad marriage in which violence was present or marital separation in order to end the violence. The majority favored the latter opinion. However, only two per cent of the pastors said they would support divorce in situations of violence.

Pastors who endorse a wife's remaining in the home until the abuse becomes "severe," and those who would not consider violence as a justification for breaking the marriage commitment, appear to hold the primacy of the marriage commitment over the sanctity of a woman's life. When such views are communicated to victims (and to victimizers), women are placed at further risk and their internal struggles are intensified. Such rigid standards for leaving increase the likelihood that a woman will either be killed by her husband, consider suicide to end the terror or adapt to the violence in some self-destructive way (for example, drug use).

Most pastors in this study indicated that they would be more than willing to accept a marriage in which some wife abuse is present—even though it is "not God's perfect will"—than they would be to advise separation, which could end in divorce. As one pastor adamantly stated, according to the New Testament "physical abuse is not grounds for divorce." Arguing similarly, a pastor from the East affirmed the church's responsibility to "uphold the sanctity of marriage. It must recognize that abuse does happen, but the church itself should do nothing that would encourage the marriage to be dissolved."

Notes

Chapter 1: A Nightmare in the Christian Home

[1]Sharon Schmickle, "Jury Finds Lucille Tisland Not Guilty," *Minneapolis Star and Tribune,* 10 March 1984.

[2]Christy F. Telch and Carol Ummerl Linquist, "Violent versus Nonviolent Couples: A Comparison of Patterns," *Psychotherapy* 21, no. 2, Summer 1984, p. 247.

Donald G. Dutton, *The Domestic Assault of Women* (Boston: Allyn and Bacon, 1988), p. 68.

[4]Cheryl Ellsworth and Irene Wagner, "Formerly Battered Women: A Follow-up Study" (Unpublished manuscript, University of Washington School of Social Work, Seattle, Washington).

[5]Richard Langley and Robert Levy, *Wife Beating: The Silent Crisis* (Boston: Beacon Press, 1983), p. 105.

[6]William A. Stacey and Anson Shupe, *The Family Secret* (Boston: Beacon Press, 1983), p. 105.

[7]Ibid., pp. 105-6.

[8]Ibid., p. 106.

Chapter 2: Who Is the Battered Woman and Why Does She Stay?

[1]Mary Gordon, *The Company of Women* (New York: Ballantine, 1980), p. 245.

[2]Langley and Levy, *Wife Beating*, p. 4.

[3]Peg Meier, "Battered in Luxury," *Minneapolis Star and Tribune*, 30 June 1988.

[4]"Wife Abuse: The Facts," *Response*, January/February 1984, p. 9.

[5]Brooks Jackson, "John Fedders of SEC Is Pummeled by Legal and Personal Problems," *The Wall Street Journal*, 25 February 1985.

[6]Charlotte Fedders and Laura Elliot, *Shattered Dreams* (New York: Harper & Row, 1987), pp. 190-191.

[7]"Wife Abuse: The Facts," p. 9.

[8]Kersti Yllo, "The Status of Women, Marital Equality, and Violence against Wives," *Journal of Family Issues* 5, no. 3 (September 1984), p. 312.

[9]Jane O'Reilly, "Wife Beating: The Silent Crime," *Time* (5 September 1983), p. 23.

[10]Department of Justice, "Report to the Nation on Crime," *Response*, January/February 1984, p. 9.

[11]Dutton, *Domestic Assault of Women*, p.18.

[12]Ibid., p. 19.

[13]Ibid., p. 20.

[14]Daniel G. Saunders, "When Battered Women Use Violence: Husband-Abuse or Self-Defense?" *Victims and Violence* 1, no. 1 (1986), pp. 47-60.

[15]Murray Straus, "Victims and Aggressors in Marital Violence," *American Behavioral Scientist* 23, no. 5 (May/June 1980), p. 691.

[16]Ibid.

[17]Lenore Walker, "The Battered Woman Syndrome Study," in David Finkelhor, Richard J. Gelles, Gerald T. Hotaling and Murray A. Straus, eds., *The Dark Side of Families* (Beverly Hills, Calif.: Sage Publications, 1983), p. 40.

[18]Terry Davidson, *Conjugal Crime* (New York: Hawthorn Books, 1978), p. 52.

[19]Richard Gelles, *The Violent Home* (Beverly Hills, Calif.: Sage Publications, 1974), p. 127.

[20]Lenore Walker, *The Battered Woman* (New York: Harper & Row, 1979), p. 22.

[21]Barbara Star, "Comparing Battered and Non-Battered Women," *Victimology* 3, nos. 1-2 (1978), p. 42.

[22]Ibid., pp. 22-23.

[23]Ibid., p. 164.

[24]Peggy Halsey, "Women in Crisis: Out There or in Here?" *Response*, June 1981, p. 5.

[25]Lenore Walker, "Battered Women and Learned Helplessness," *Victimology* 2,

nos. 3-4 (1977-78), p. 528.

[26]Diane Mundt, "Man Charged in Attack on Ex-Wife, Her Neighbor," *Minneapolis Star and Tribune*, 21 May 1986.

[27]"Understanding Domestic Violence," *Radix*, March/April 1984, pp. 14-20.

[28]Steven Morgan, *Conjugal Terrorism: A Psychological and Community Treatment Model of Wife Abuse* (Palo Alto, Calif.: R & E Research Associates, 1982), p. 30.

[29]Debra S. Kalmuss and Murray A. Straus, "Wife's Marital Dependency and Wife Abuse," *Journal of Marriage and the Family* 44, no. 2 (May 1982), pp. 277, 284.

[30]James C. Dobson, *Love Must Be Tough* (Waco, Tex.: Word, 1983), p. 150.

[31]Walker, *Battered Woman*, p. 152.

[32]Walker, "Battered Women Syndrome Study," p. 43.

Chapter 3: What Kind of Men Abuse Their Wives?

[1]Paul Tournier, *The Violence Within* (New York: Harper & Row, 1978), p. 10.

[2]Richard Cohen, "Men Have Buddies, But No Real Friends," *Networker*, January/February 1985, pp. 4-5.

[3]Personal interview, 10 July 1982.

[4]Michael Wicks, "A Batterer's Perspective" (Minneapolis: Domestic Abuse Project), p. 2.

[5]Lenore Walker, "Treatment Alternatives for Battered Women," in J. R. Chapman and M. Gates, eds., *The Victimization of Women* (Beverly Hills, Calif.: Sage Publications, 1978), p. 146.

[6]Walker, "Battered Woman Syndrome Study," pp. 37-38.

[7]M. F. Hirsch, *Women and Violence* (New York: Van Nostrand Reinhold, 1981), p. 175.

[8]Richard J. Gelles, "An Exchange/Social Control Theory," Finkelhor et al., eds., *Dark Side of Families*, p. 152.

[9]Telch and Linquist, "Violent versus Nonviolent Couples," p. 247.

[10]R. A. Berk, S. F. Berk, D. R. Loseke and D. Rauma, "Mutual Combat and Other Family Violence Myths," Finkelhor et al., eds., *Dark Side of Families*, pp. 197-212.

[11]Wicks, "A Batterer's Perspective."

[12]Quotations by Dan Keller were taken from a phone interview conducted November 1988.

[13]Quotations by Paul Hegstrom were taken from a phone interview conducted November 1988 and from "Battered Families: Help and Hope," a "Focus on the Family" radio program aired March 24 and 25, 1988. Information about the Domestic Violence Learning Center can be obtained by writing to Box

3743, Quincy, Illinois 62305 or by calling 217/222-3711.

[14]Albert R. Roberts, "Intervention with the Abusive Partner," in Albert R. Roberts, ed., *Battered Women and Their Families* (New York: Springer, 1984), p. 89.

[15]Grant L. Martin, *Counseling for Family Violence and Abuse* (Waco, Tex.: Word Books, 1987), p. 98.

[16]Ibid., p. 99.

[17]Ibid., p. 100.

[18]Roberts, "Intervention," p. 114.

[19]Dutton, *Domestic Assault of Women*, p. 169.

[20]Ibid.

[21]Ibid., p. 110.

[22]Ibid., p. 114.

Chapter 4: Evil: The Heart of Violence

[1]Rex Beaber, "Conversations with Killers: Is Evil Loose in the World?" *Los Angeles Times*, 9 January 1985.

[2]Charles Colson, "The Problem of Power," *Jubilee*, July 1984, p. 3.

[3]Richard Foster, *Money, Sex & Power* (San Francisco: Harper & Row, 1983), p. 157.

[4]Ibid., p. 180.

[5]Tournier, *Violence Within*, p. 40.

[6]Edward E. Ericson, Jr., *Solzhenitsyn: The Moral Vision* (Grand Rapids, Mich.: Eerdmans, 1980), p. 9.

[7]Ibid., p. 50.

[8]Ibid., p. 57.

[9]Ibid., p. 76.

[10]Ericson, *Solzhenitsyn*, pp. 168-69.

[11]M. Scott Peck, *People of the Lie* (New York: Simon and Schuster, 1983), p. 42.

Chapter 5: Blaming the Victim

[1]Tournier, *Violence Within*, p. 23.

[2]Letty Cottin Pogrebin, "Do Women Make Men Violent?" *Ms.*. November 1974, p. 80.

[3]"Beloved Unbeliever," a radio interview by Dr. James Dobson with Jo Berry on "Focus on the Family," November 1984.

[4]Jeffrey A. Fagen, Douglas K. Stewart and Karen V. Hanse, "Violent Men or Violent Husbands?" Finkelhor et al., eds., *Dark Side of Families*, p. 57.

[5]James Dobson, *Love Must Be Tough* (Waco, Tex.: Word, 1986), pp. 24-25.

6Ibid., pp. 148-49.

7Ibid., p. 149.

8Ibid., pp. 146-50.

9Ibid., pp. 149-50.

10"Battered Families: Help and Hope," a radio interview with Paul and Judy Hegstrom and Heidi by Dr. James Dobson on "Focus on the Family," aired March 24 and 25, 1988.

11Ibid.

12William Ryan, *Blaming the Victim* (New York: Vintage Books, 1971), p. 8.

13R. Emerson Dobash and Russell Dobash, *Violence against Wives,* (New York: The Free Press, 1979), p. 160.

14Susan Brownmiller, *Against Our Will* (New York: Simon and Schuster, 1975), p. 315.

15*Random House Dictionary, Unabridged* (New York: Random House, 1967).

16Anna F. Kuhl, "Personality Traits of Abused Women: Masochism Myth Refuted," *Victimology* 9, nos. 3-4 (1984), p. 461.

17Paula Caplan, "The Myth of Women's Masochism," *American Psychologist* 39, no. 2 (February 1984), pp. 134-35.

18Walker, *Battered Woman,* p. 29.

19Walker, "Battered Women and Learned Helplessness," p. 526.

20Walker, *Battered Woman,* p. 50.

21O'Reilly, "Wife Beating," p. 23.

22Paul Meier and Frank Minirth, *Happiness Is a Choice* (Grand Rapids, Mich.: Baker, 1978), pp. 96-97.

23Davidson, *Conjugal Crime,* p. 204.

24Dobash and Dobash, *Violence against Wives,* p. 145.

25Kathleen J. Ferraro, "Rationalizing Violence: How Battered Women Stay," *Victimology* 11 (1986), pp. 203-12.

26Susan Thistlethwaite, "Battered Women and the Bible: From Subjection to Liberation," *Christianity and Crisis* 41, no. 18, p. 311.

Chapter 6: Wife Abuse and the Submission of Women

1Gretchen Gaebelein Hull, *Equal to Serve* (New Jersey: Revell, 1987), p. 200.

2Peter W. Keely, "Who Speaks for God?" an unpublished paper.

3Elizabeth Rice Handford, *Me? Obey Him?* (Murfreesboro, Tenn.: Sword of the Lord, 1972), p. 28.

4From an address by Reverend Joy Bussert, given at a conference on "Battering: Looking at the Church's Response," Oak Grove Presbyterian Church, Bloomington, Minnesota, 28 February 1984.

5Megan Jobling, "Battered Wives: A Survey," *Social Service Quarterly* 47

(1974), p. 82.

[6]George Thorman, *Family Violence* (Springfield, Ill.: Charles C. Thomas, 1980), p. 119.

[7]Walker, *Battered Woman*, pp. 22-23.

[8]"U.S. Says Women Who Report Abuse Lower Odds They'll Be Attacked Again," *Minneapolis Star and Tribune*, 18 August 1986.

[9]Marvin De Hann, "Have You Excommunicated Your Spouse?" *Good News Broadcaster*, March 1982, p. 47.

[10]John MacArthur, *The Family* (Chicago: Moody Press, 1982), p. 18.

[11]John Dart, "Woman's Place Is at Home, Pastor Says," *Los Angeles Times*, 1982.

[12]MacArthur, *The Family*, p. 31.

[13]Ibid., p. 47.

[14]Ibid., p. 28.

[15]Ibid., p. 53.

[16]Paul Meier and Richard Meier, *Family Foundations* (Grand Rapids, Mich.: Baker, 1981), p. 106.

[17]Paul Meier, Frank Minirth and Frank Wichern, *Introduction to Psychology & Counseling* (Grand Rapids, Mich.: Baker, 1982), p. 363.

[18]Ibid., p. 369.

[19]Clyde Narramore, *The Submissive Wife* (Rosemead, Calif.: Narramore Christian Foundation, 1978), pp. 14-15.

[20]Bill Gothard, *Supplementary Alumni Book*, vol. 5 (Institute in Basic Youth Conflicts, 1979), p. 10.

[21]Ibid., p. 1.

[22]Virginia Mollenkott, "Dialogue with Bill Gothard," *Faith at Work*, 1975, p. 26.

[23]Susan T. Foh, *Women and the Word of God: A Response to Biblical Feminism* (Grand Rapids, Mich.: Baker, 1980), p. 88.

[24]Meier, Minirth and Wichern, *Introduction*, p. 383.

[25]Hull, *Equal to Serve*.

[26]Ibid., p. 200.

[27]S. Scott Bartchy, "Power, Submission, and Sexual Identity among the Early Christians," in Roberta Hestenes, comp., *Women and Men in Ministry* (Fuller Theological Seminary, 1984), pp. 114-15.

[28]Ibid., p. 103.

[29]Ibid., pp. 114-15.

[30]Richard J. Foster, *The Celebration of Discipline* (San Francisco: Harper & Row, 1978), p. 104.

[31]Berkeley and Alvera Mickelsen, "The Head of the Epistles," *Christianity To-*

day, 20 February 1981, p. 20.

[32]Ibid.

[33]Ibid., p. 22.

[34]David Finkelhor, "Common Features of Family Abuse," Finkelhor et al., eds., *Dark Side of Families,* p. 18.

[35]Jean Giles-Sims, *Wife-Battering* (New York: The Guilford Press, 1983).

[36]Yllo, "Status of Women," pp. 316-17.

[37]Murray A. Straus, Richard J. Gelles and Suzanne K. Steinmetz, *Behind Closed Doors: Violence in the American Family* (Garden City, Calif.: Anchor Books, 1980), p. 193.

[38]Ibid.

[39]Ibid.

[40]Jean Baker-Miller, *Toward a New Psychology of Women* (Boston, Mass.: Beacon Press, 1976), p. 12.

[41]Ibid., p. 15.

[42]Ibid., p. 9.

[43]Ibid., p. 7.

[44]Ibid., p. 19.

[45]Ibid., pp. 60, 25-26.

Chapter 7: The Process of Reconciliation

[1]Lewis Smedes, *Forgive and Forget* (San Francisco: Harper & Row, 1984), p. 94.

[2]Lynn Buzzard, "Reconciliation: A Limited Warranty and Disclosure Statement," *Theology, News and Notes* (Fuller Theological Seminary, March 1985), pp. 23, 26.

[3]Desmond Tutu, "The Processes of Reconciliation and the Demand of Obedience," *Transformation* 3, no. 6 (April/June 1986), p. 6.

[4]Smedes, *Forgive and Forget,* p. 18.

[5]Buzzard, "Reconciliation," p. 22.

[6]Foster, *Celebration of Discipline,* pp. 4-5.

[7]Dietrich Bonhoeffer, *The Cost of Discipleship* (New York: Macmillan Publishing Co., 1963), pp. 57, 47.

[8]Ibid., p. 76.

[9]Foster, *Celebration of Discipline,* p. 6.

[10]Smedes, *Forgive and Forget,* p. 44.

[11]Ibid., pp. 134, 39, 49.

[12]Ibid., p. 81.

[13]Anne Rood, "Looking the Snake in the Eye," *Jubilee,* January 1986, p. 1.

[14]Ibid., p. 67.

[15]Karl Menninger, *Whatever Became of Sin?* (New York: Hawthorne Books, 1973), pp. 177, 179-80.

[16]Ibid., pp. 67-68.

[17]Lewis Okun, *Woman Abuse* (Albany, New York: State University of New York Press, 1986).

Chapter 8: Marriage, Divorce and Wife Abuse

[1]George Levinger, "Sources of Marital Dissatisfaction among Applicants for Divorce," *American Journal of Orthopsychiatry* 36 (1966), pp. 803-7.

[2]Ray S. Anderson, "The Purpose of Marriage as an Expression of Love and Sexuality," *Essays on Social Theology of the Family* (Fuller Theological Seminary, August 1984), p. 136.

[3]Ibid.

[4]Evelyn Eaton Whitehead and James D. Whitehead, *Marrying Well* (New York: Doubleday, 1981), pp. 351-52.

[5]Lewis B. Smedes, *Mere Morality* (Grand Rapids, Mich.: Eerdmans, 1983), p. 163.

[6]Foster, *Money, Sex & Power*, p. 145.

[7]Ibid., p. 144.

[8]Allen Verhey, "Divorce and the New Testament," *Reformed Journal,* May/June 1976, p. 19.

[9]Ibid., p. 30.

[10]Anderson, "Purpose of Marriage," p. 141.

[11]"Requests to Remarry: The Pastors' Catch-22," *Leadership Journal* 4, no. 3 (1983), p. 120.

[12]Ibid., pp. 111-21.

Chapter 9: The Church and Reconciliation

[1]Buzzard, "Reconciliation."

[2]Paul Jewett, *Theology, News and Notes,* March 1985, p. 20.

[3]Buzzard, "Reconciliation," p. 22.

[4]Jose Miqeues Bonino, *Doing Theology in a Revolutionary Situation* (New York: Seabury, 1974), p. 120.

[5]Smedes, *Mere Morality,* p. 27.

[6]Davidson, *Conjugal Crime,* p. 17.

[7]Bonhoeffer, *Cost of Discipleship,* p. 69.

[8]From a survey on wife abuse conducted by Elaine Storkey for "Men, Women and God," London Institute for Contemporary Christianity, St. Peter's Church, Vere Street, London W1M 9HP.

[9]Tutu, "Processes of Reconciliation," p. 4.

[10]Davidson, *Conjugal Crime,* p. 228.

[11]Elizabeth Hilberman and Kit Munson, "Sixty Battered Women," *Victimology* 2, nos. 3-4 (1977-78), pp. 460-70.

[12]Davidson, *Conjugal Crime,* pp. 206-7.

[13]Stacey and Shupe, *Family Secret,* p. 105.

[14]R. F. Mollica, F. J. Streets and F. C. Redlich, "A Community Study of Formal Pastoral Counseling Activities of the Clergy," *American Journal of Psychiatry* 143, no. 3 (March 1986), pp. 323-28.

[15]James M. Alsdurf, "Wife Abuse and Christian Faith: An Assessment of the Church's Response" (a dissertation presented to the Graduate School of Psychology, Fuller Theological Seminary, April 1985).

[16]National Association of Evangelicals Task Force on the Family, 1985.

[17]R. Emerson Dobash and Russell Dobash, "Wives: The 'appropriate' victims of marital violence," *Victimology* 2, nos. 3-4 (1977-78), p. 430.

[18]Terry Davidson, "Wifebeating: A Recurring Phenomenon throughout History," in Maria Roy, ed., *Battered Women* (New York: Van Nostrand Reinhold, 1977), p. 4.

[19]L. Martines and J. O'Faolain, *Not in God's Image* (New York: Harper & Row, 1973).

[20]Davidson, *Conjugal Crime,* p. 98.

[21]"Straight Talk from Ben Kinchlow," *Family Life Today,* March 1986, p. 21.

[22]Hull, *Equal To Serve,* p. 198.

[23]Richard Nardwind, "Date Beating: What Study Found about Violence and Teens," *Los Angeles Herald-Examiner,* 16 September 1983.

[24]"Courtship Violence Touches 1 in 6, College Survey Shows," *Minneapolis Star and Tribune,* 7 January 1984.

[25]Paul Levy, "Courtship Often a Violent Time, St. Cloud Study Finds," *Minneapolis Star and Tribune,* 12 February 1984, p. 14f.

[26]Berkeley Mickelsen and Alvera Mickelsen, "Does Male Dominance Tarnish Our Translations?" *Christianity Today,* 5 October 1979, p. 25.

[27]Ibid., p. 26.

[28]John Johnsson, "When You Put Your Body Where Your Mouth Is," *Transformation* 3, no. 2 (April/June 1986), p. 39.

Conclusion: Violence in the Land

[1]Joyce Sunila, *Los Angeles Times,* 24 July 1983.

[2]Julia London, "Images of Violence against Women," *Victimology* 2, nos. 3-4 (1977-78), p. 518.

[3]Karen Lindsey, *Friends as Family* (Boston: Beacon Press, 1981), p. 2.

[4]Stacey and Shupe, *Family Secret,* pp. 7-8.

[5]Russ Chandler, "Southern Baptist Delegates Reject Ordination of Women," *Minneapolis Star and Tribune*, 16 June 1984.

[6]Davidson, *Conjugal Crime*, p. 97.

[7]Davidson, "Wifebeating," p. 7.

[8]Christine Buchholy, *Marriage and Divorce Today* 8, no. 23 (10 January 1978).

[9]Henri J. M. Nouwen, "Creating True Intimacy," *Sojourners*, June 1985, p. 15.

[10]Baker-Miller, *Toward a New Psychology of Women*, p. 13.

[11]Ibid.

Appendix: The Response of the Clergy to the Problem of Wife Abuse
[1]Alsdurf, "Wife Abuse and Christian Faith."